AF663343

Parivarthana

The Change

notionpress
.com

Parivarthana
The Change

A M Nagesh

notionpress.com

Notion Press

Old No. 38, New No. 6

McNichols Road, Chetpet

Chennai - 600 031

First Published by Notion Press 2016

Copyright © A M Nagesh 2016

All Rights Reserved.

ISBN 978-93-5206-863-0

This book has been published in good faith that the work of the author is original. All efforts have been taken to make the material error-free. However, the author and the publisher disclaim the responsibility.

No part of this book may be used, reproduced in any manner whatsoever without written permission from the author, except in the case of brief quotations embodied in critical articles and reviews.

Dedicated to
My Mother

Humility is a divine flight, across earth to heaven, we wait to board, to find empty chairs, expecting to get filled up only in vain, left our heart heavy, nothing sooths except waiting…waiting…waiting…

– Dr A M Nagesh

Contents

PREFACE

Our misery today is because of two reasons. One is due to lack of insight and the other is due to want of enlightenment. If we take a 'U' turn and slightly vary our insight that misery can be mystery, it will enable us to travel towards mysticism. If we take time to accept and understand this insight, it is a definite path towards nano enlightenment but it need not be total enlightenment. I do not have both, but recently I have borrowed them. Insight and enlightenment are valued most and are not available in the market as a commodity. When both are not available, I could not anyway possess them. I have undertaken an affirmative path, in which insight is a near possibility but not enlightenment. In my heydays, both were impossible to acquire due to many reasons. One reason was my self-sustaining obsessions. Of late, I have a lot of time on my hands due to a relaxed lifestyle at my age. My time could be spent in meeting friends and talking irrelevant things or going to many clubs and consuming alcoholic drinks. Both are deterring factors for my health and also for acquiring knowledge. Nowadays, many *swamijis*, preachers and soothsayers are growing in number. They have become famous and filled their pockets with money. In fact, I found spirituality to be the main reason behind their success. As a practicing psychiatrist, I pondered on this phenomenon. From that moment, I became a seeker, seeking or visualising our club's alcoholic drinks as an inspiration for spirituality. At this juncture, my friend, who is a doctor and practices near to my clinic, presented a book on basic ways of learning insight. He said, "Reading this book will help you to counsel your patients better." His counsel worked, and it ignited my insight. From that day, there were several alterations in me, and in the meantime, it also was a platform for me to heal. Slowly, I started collecting many books in relation to my interest. Reading these books created an interest in me to delve deeper into this field. While doing so, I formed my own concepts regarding certain words that are regularly used by us without knowing what they actually mean. Working on those concepts, I began to relate science, society, environment and man. Ultimately, I found no difference among them; everything looked "one" to me. That is why I love Buddha, who explained the cosmic web of interconnection, inter-relation and inter-dependence. Today, physicists are trying to unravel his teachings scientifically.

ACKNOWLEDGMENTS

It is not fair on my part to forget my aunt, late Smt Sathya Susheelamma, with whom I stayed for two years, and who helped me morally and financially during my Pre University College (PUC) days, as well as during my under-graduation days.

I also wish to pay my homage to my uncle, late Sri C V Anantha Narayana Shetty (Mannars, Mysore). Without his guidance, I would not have joined MBBS.

I joined psychiatry in NIMHANS after reading a small psychiatry textbook that was given to me by my late Prof Dr Sathyanarayana Swamy. I pay my homage to him too.

I profusely thank all my teachers for the knowledge they imparted throughout my life, for teaching me at each step and making me to write this book, which to me was a mirage come true. Many such teachers have reached their heavenly abode; to them also I pay my homage.

I acknowledge and appreciate my wife, Smt Chaya, for all the pains she took to enable me to fulfil my obsession of bringing out this book. I love my children, Dr Manu and Dr Dhanya, for their criticisms and corrections.

My writings are not intended to hurt or offend anyone, directly or indirectly, and my book is merely an educative book for the reader.

It is Mr Chinnehalli Swamy, my lab technician, a Kannada literature passionate, who forced me to take up writing because of my interest in ancient scriptures.

I thank all my relatives, especially my uncle Sri K. V. Vasudev Murthy (retired district judge, retired secretary, Legal aid, Lokayuktha, Karnataka). My humble thanks are due to my doctor friends who helped me with all their love during my difficult days. In addition, I heartily thank those who helped in making this book come alive.

–Dr A M Nagesh

THE WORLD OF WEIRD QUESTIONS

In this weird world, weird people raise weird questions like:

"Doctor, why should a baby be born only at the end of nine months? Why not at five months?"

"Why is the sky blue and not yellow?"

During my under-graduation days, I had a friend, who, whenever we met, would ask me these sorts of questions. He was a trouble monger, always asking weird questions to his friends. My friends used to avoid him; in spite of that, he always managed to question us until we left college. In truth, I do not have any answer to his questions. In my view, for many such simple questions, we do not have the correct answers. Probably scientists might provide some relevant answers, though not complete explanations. Many a time, the answers by the scientists confuse ordinary men. Still, scientists are able to provide answers for many such weird questions through their sheer intelligence; they invariably think themselves superior to others, and hence their ego. Ordinary men are contrary to this; they are ignorant, pious and simple in nature because they understand and appreciate only simple answers. These simple answers from ordinary men are more philosophical and unscientific, and hence vague in their presentation. They attribute all the happenings in this world to the power of God (God Saibaba weeping or offering *Vibhuthi* from his portraits). We have a group of people who are neither scientists nor ordinary men but are quite articulate in their answers; they blend science and philosophy and form their own theories. They answer all types of questions. When we question them on various concerns, such as, when will I marry? When will I get money? When will I have children and when will I die?, we get beautiful, promising and exciting answers. In my country, knowledgeable people listen to them and become poor in their thoughts, as well as with their money. Irrespective of intelligentsia and ignorance, such foolish questions keep cropping up every day in different dimensions. Intelligent people might find a scientific answer to all these imperative questions. Later, these answers find meaning to fictional questions, which might become true in our future life. The ignorant and cheated never find proper answers to such questions; they silently keep listening to these answers and remain quiet, as they would have lost every significant feature in their life, monetarily, psychologically and materially. For me, there is one such forsaken group comprising extremely mentally retarded people, who are actually God-like, and are baffled by the above questions and answers, as they have nothing to take nor give to the world.

QUANTUM THEORY

I have a theory for the reader; this theory may appear a little bit absurd. Under this theory, man who looks smart superficially may not be truc inside. In search of this truth, I have one question to be asked. What is the "absolute" or the "truth?" *Guru* said, "Absolute is zero"; in reality, this truth does not hold good. In our interaction, we must realise that in the ordinary world this zero has no value but the same zero in the mathematical world has enormous value. For a man with *Vedanthic* integrity, this zero is everything and also bliss. If this logic is true, then truth has to be absolute. At practical levels, in this present world, possessing that total truthfulness is impossible. Hence, presently truth is in a relative state when its practicality and its applications to the society are considered. If this statement is correct, then truth is always elusive. Therefore, truth is always fluctuating, with its own forward momentum. If I am right in this philosophy, the just narrated concept of mine fits into quantum theory. The quantum theory narrates antigravity and inconsistent properties of a matter, which are both opposite to the general thinking in physics. Hence, the same principle holds good for my truth. Understandably, my truth is never situated at the centre; this truth is always present at the periphery. Bringing this truth to the centre is a hazardous process and is painful for an individual. No one in this world likes the truth and still everyone lives with that truth in different dimensions and proportions. When I say Truth is an action, it is just an act at the periphery; at the centre, it is untruthfulness to this justifiable act. All of us know that to be truthful is a difficult proposition. If somebody says that he sticks only to the truth, definitely I am sure that he is lying. This is like to a state where if somebody is angry, he cannot say that 'I am changed to no anger' state. This is not possible because anger stays with him forever. Buddha had anger; he had never said he without anger. He just accepted his anger and transcended it. This process of transcendence took many years of realisation and understanding. Mahan Buddha spent 20 years of his lifetime only on meditation and silence. He said, "Not to fight with anger or no anger, truth or no truth, just accept the anger and also the truth, then try to live always with them at the centre and not at the periphery. The struggle to fight within the anger less or truthless state is an enormous process, which requires lots of knowledge. With that state, people are near to the truth, but may not be inside the truth." It was the story of the past; now, the world has changed. The world is full of fast and small things. Life is more robotic and mechanical. For a meaningful life, what we require today is only one minute of silence, and from this silence, we can prevent many suicides, homicides and also evil worldly happenings. This is what Buddha called as *Samyama* (patience)

What do our present-day saints do? They keep on struggling within their mind (sketch) only to cheat and appear pious for their followers outside. Buddha was the opposite; he fought this anger inside. He never said we should not fight anger, he asked us to fight the same inside with acceptance. That was his *Manthra.* When we accept our anger and also someone else's anger we go directly in to a state of silence because we are already there or we are in that centre of anger. In this stage, we do not fight. Hence, realisation and understanding of life leads us to the silence. Buddha said, "To accept it as it is (*Thathatha*)."

The periphery is always noisy, as in an idealistic man. They keep on bombarding everyone around them with their ideals, thus creating an atmosphere of fear leading to much new sectarianism. We might agree to the point that at certain times an idealistic man could cause a cheater to trick the innocent people around him. Hence, to have a peaceful life, we have to drop the just mentioned constructs at the periphery; hence, for the peace to come in our midst, we have to adopt acceptance, and by doing so, the mind inside us is illuminated; thus, the inside light brightens the dark outside. Finding the illuminated spiritual world inside and also finding the bright environment outside would allow us to enjoy the possible bliss.

MY KARMA

Many *Vedanta* books are loaded with answers regarding questions like: am I immortal? The simple answer would be that the body is mortal but deeds are immortal. What remains permanently are the good remnants of our good work. This has been explained in the *Karma* Theory. This concept is accepted all over the world by enlightened people who have orientation towards Hindu Philosophy. Theologists and meta physicists are also of the same opinion irrespective of their religion. This is our style of preaching; but at present, God men's preaching is differing a little bit. They explain, "Have good account, never spend and leave everything down here, and by doing so you can attain *Moksha* (panacea)." That is how in our country modern Swamis have amassed money. From all such consultations, they collect exorbitant fees and enjoy all pleasures of life.

SPECK IN THIS UNIVERSE

We all are attracted towards gold, which always glitters; meanwhile, we fail to realise that there also exists a new world within the glittering matter that is really a heaven worth visiting. This is possible by an atomist after splitting the matter to atoms in his laboratory, but for a seeker like me, it is possible by guessing the amazing atomic world. While acquiring such knowledge slowly and partially, I found out that we are all living on a dust-like particle. What is this dust then? For me, this earth is a speck or nano-like fragment of this huge universe; hence, earth is a speck out of a dust particle thrown out from a common source of tremendous explosion that happened billions of years ago. The paradox is that our origin is from this tremendous explosion; it is unfortunate to know that our destruction today is also by powerful explosions by our numerous terrorist outfits. These outfit's roots are so strong and deep that we are unable to uproot them. These roots have been fed with nourishing nutrients by appeasing politics, by fundamental fanatics, by religious right wings, by local sympathisers and also from pseudo-secular human activists. Hence, the stem of this tree is so strong that even America's dirty bomb is not able to destroy them. The treatment is possible only when we have deep understanding, compassionate approach and empathetic looks with sympathy. It is possible when our social in-equalities are met properly all over the world especially by the leading countries. Our approach in this line should not be paranoia, it should be from the heart with full transparency and right action.

For us this earth appears big, but when we tend to travel hundred billion light years away in this huge universe, our earth looks invisible. The same is true for a specially designed intelligent alien, if at all he exists hundred billion light years away. This appears to be more fictional and hypothetical; we do not know the alien existence precisely. Let us imagine our existence if the said hypothesis is true. In that state, we are all sub-atomic particles like protons and neutrons for them. In fact, the earth is derived from protons and neutrons (plasma). We have tried to recreate matter but have failed miserably to get one God Particle. Experiments are yet going on to get the Higgs Boson particle, but when? God only knows. We know the Big Bang occurred a long time back just like that; we are also living just like that and are surviving just like that. Any amount of explanation or knowledge regarding this phenomenon cannot explain the process of life's origin.

HAPPINESS

When we try to look at ourselves, it is wonderful to find different looks and different mind sets, unlike frogs and fishes of the same species that differ only in size, which depends on their years of existence. They find each other with god-given scent; in men, identification is by our looks. Frogs and fishes fight for their survival, we fight for attachments. Survival and attachments are dangerous. Deep down in the heart, we do not find happiness from both. Science exists only on definitions. Today, psychology also has been viewed as a science. Here, definitions for many psychological terms are vague. For me, the question, "what is happiness?" amuses me the most; this happiness is a relative concept rather than an absolute concept; 'happy' at one stage may not be so at another stage. What is happy for me may not be so for the other person. Hence, with this diversity, happiness is not available in the market. It belongs to each individual with a particular framework, where greed and possessiveness are least prevalent. Hence, happiness differs from each individual. When we take any happy construct with the individuals, they have their own particular framework, in which the other opposite constructs play a minimal role. Then how could this minimum happiness is achieved by an individual? Yes, happiness could be achieved in many ways, but to say a few, it is in one's biology or hereditary components, environmental upbringing, school and peer factors, knowledge acquired and by understanding the pulse of our life. In humans, knowledgeable thinking has been defined in different perspectives; one such definition is inward journey or spiritual thinking, another by the way of outward journey or scientific thinking.

GOD

Leaving spiritual and scientific things apart, have we tried to understand our origin? This is a foremost basic question for an evolutionist. As I am not an evolutionist, the answer for this question appears complicated, so to make it simple, I can wash off my hands by saying "God's creation." Then who is God? If creation is not by God then from whom, whether it could be from some kind of spirit, and if so, what is spirit? These sorts of questions keep arising, but ultimately no answers are obtained. The answers do differ from each individual without arriving at a single conclusion. The answer depends on each person's different backgrounds, which I have already mentioned. My friend asked me, can you explain God? When many cannot explain God, how can I answer? Let me give a possible explanation rather than a definition.

"God is as follows" I told him. "What does 'G' stands for? It stands for geological, then 'O' is read as organised; then what is 'D' meant for? It is meant for developed." Now combine all these three and observe. After this observation, one would view origin of life as geologically organised and developed organisms. Hence, if this logic is correct then, "I am God." The great saint *Adi Shankaracharya* held this view when he said *aham brahmasmi.* According to science, is it not true? If we ask a science student, he would give similar answers. As per the evolution theory, we all have been born out from nature's struggle. This is the reason why we worship Nature as *Panchabhuthas;* they are five in number. These are water, soil, air, fire and sky (space). This has been well depicted in our old scriptures *(*Puranas*)* as in the hypothetical churning of fantasy milk sea *(Samudra Mantana).* For years and years, five stupid brothers fought and fought to produce one living particle called amino acid. The different amino acids got mixed, survived, escaped the fury of nature, became intelligent and that is how now we see ourselves as ours and not as Nature's gift. Mother Nature gifted it to us, and at the same time, we began to conquer Mother Nature in return. We spit, we tear her clothes and put plastic cover over her body. We have gagged her, we have suffocated her, we have sucked water from her and we have allowed her to starve. We have systematically destroyed her minerals. If this is the true story, what sort of bones she can possess? She is actually crippling. We have made her bones to suffer from iatrogenic disease called "osteoporosis" where in this condition her bones just cannot bear our weight anymore. She will buckle to the present man made trends for us to suffer in no time. We should be spiritual to overcome this by way of changing our attitude to prevent her from man made disasters so that She would allow us to survive calmly hereafter.

SPIRIT AT ITS TRUE SENSE

My late grandfather was a spiritual man. He had obsessions and compulsions that he owed money to certain native gods; he had a habit of disbursing money to many nearby temples unnecessarily. To my innocent question regarding God, he would explain with a simple answer as 'spirituality.' This answer from my grandfather began to bother me till very recently when I thought of writing a book on few concepts of my interest. Is this spirituality a type of alcohol or some kind of potion? I have my own way of explaining this spirituality. In medicine, we have a medicine for all diseases alike when we are not in a position to diagnose a particular disease. We have a drug called steroids where it is tried on a trial and error basis. This said drug is otherwise called *Ramabana* (Lord Rama's arrow that killed Ravana the demon) or *Amrutha* (a sacred potion that on drinking provides immortality). Ordinary men shun doctors because doctors are more expensive and so they find cheap *Ramabana* for their innumerable sorrows. Before discussing spirituality, concentrate on my narration.

To run our brain we require electricity; hence, the creator is careful enough to provide a carbon battery and also a carbon chip, which is programmed by Him for our lifetime, say for hundred years if everything goes fine. If the brain does not produce electricity, then that brain is dead. In this state, internal organs are perfectly alright and these organs can be used for organ transplantations.

This happens in accidents where there is severe injury to the brain. Some are fortunate to have good batteries and others are run by average batteries. Many of us are not charged well at first instant; charging depends upon many factors like one's bio-socio, cultural and educational background. Majority of us are not fortunate enough to inherit such great qualities. Today, people endowed with such qualities exploit others and people who have not been granted with those qualities suffer. Therefore, happiness and sorrow coexist. Both are painful; hence, people want to relieve from their pain with some kind of medicine. To cheat a person is not that easy because the cheaters' *Athma* would not allow him to become a bad man. Hence, to cheat, he has to take some kind of alcohol to muffle his good sense and so also to cover his conscious, *Athma*. The men who are cheated by such men have to take this alcohol to get over their depression. Doctors, as I mentioned earlier, are always expensive. Hence, the cheapest would be the spirit or alcohol, which is available on the roadside. After consumption of this divine-healing liquid called alcohol, it instantly tranquilises the disturbed mind. The same spirit makes a person to talk if he does not talk; this also makes a person to do particular acts, if he does not do them. The strong spirit would knock down a hyperactive or excited man. Therefore, this alcohol has many functions in its capacity. That is why it is otherwise called *Ramabana,* which killed Ravana. This is exactly what I want to convey.

By the above narration, we learnt that this spirit produces bad and also good effects. Then what does actually 'spirituality' say? The answer is simple; the tranquillity of mind one obtains without consuming the alcohol or related substances is called spirituality or the study of good effects of spirit or alcohol without the consumption of spirit or alcohol is called spirituality. This answer confuses the reader. Yes, it is always confusing as I explained in the beginning. Spirituality has been related to God but I am relating it with this alcohol available on the roadside bars. Once again, I will make a point to the confused reader. "Studying the good qualities of a person after he attains knowledge through learned means and also experiencing the happiness that he obtains after such readings is called spirituality. The happiness and the experience what he obtains should not be secondary to any drug or intoxicant use." I hope I have explained it clearly. Therefore, this spirituality is not the asset of any swamis or self-proclaimed god-like people. Understanding this spiritual nature requires extra effort to study, hard persuasion to understand, more practice to follow and lot of patience to realise. If we try to watch this world carefully, many problems we are facing today are not by ordinary men but by learned men who have strong egos attached like a monkey tail. Because of this monkey tail, many behave like monkeys after taking alcohol or spirit. So the spirit what I am talking about is not true liquid spirit but a hypothetical divine spirit. It is a spirit in its true sense required by all to learn and to impart goodness. This type of spirit should be taught at the grass root levels; these teachings should be inculcated in our syllabus at our primary school levels. This teaching should not be contaminated; it should be crystal clear, so that the students should not be put to unnecessary confusion. The information what a student gets from schools should be true to its spirit and possess real facts. If we see the curriculum in Buddha land, the grass root level teaching is meditation and then books. In our land, it is books first and meditation last.

Well, will this type of teaching help in lifting our dharma? No, it never has happened until now. Initially we are taught Gandhian principles, when we put the same principles in this present society later, these Gandhian principles play no role. People should realise that we cannot get spirituality by visiting temples, offering our woes to imaginary gods and listening to cheaters or bad preachers. The spirit should come within us; it should get doubly saturated by our knowledge acquisition and through our learning process. So, this spirituality could be obtained simply through mere observations by the students. The observation made by the student should be moulded and promoted by good teachers, but unfortunately, many teachers do not know when, where and by whom the Dandi movement was held in our country.

SATTHA

High intelligence or highly charged batteries do not work in this present world. The world is filled with ordinary men or common batteries. What the ordinary man requires are common requirements. To write in simple words, food, clothe and shelter *(Roti, Kapada Aur Makan)*. If this basic *Sattha* (human rights) is not provided then the ordinary man become rebellious. Till now, such type of full blown rebellious attitude has not been seen in our people. In our country, all of us have imbibed innate extraordinary tolerance through our genes. These innate tolerances have been exploited by our *Netas*. Because of this, we have remained poor even after sixty-six years of independence not by money but psychologically. Depending on one's quality of expression and artistic nature, a person can reach a celebrity status. I am not against any celebrity or big politician; as any common man, I expect them to execute a few moral standards. Moral is, let them keep their status or ego at par with common men. If he does not shed the ego, he will not become eternal as his hoarded money left on earth for his bystanders to use. After spending this money, bystanders either remember or worship this person who is no more. I call them as great philanthropists *(Maha Danis)*. They neither enjoy nor share their enjoyments with others while living. Hence, they leave everything for strangers to enjoy. At least, let them do something with that hoarded money so that this money would be useful in the society, let this money not go waste like unclaimed deposits at banks. The most unfortunate part of our present scenario is that the public memory is proverbially short. It is this factor that has helped the unethical *Neta*s to get away with their misdeeds with impunity and the present-day *Neta* allowing the elector to suffer.

BEND

Once I met a tall person and walking along with him made me appear small. I felt I was inferior to him and at the same time a thought came to my mind that walking tall and straight would lead to many problems. A tall person would hurt his head while entering a temple's sanctum sanctorum. A tall man hurts his head entering his small car, which might leave him dizzy as he avoids big cars due to parking owes. If he is straight and tall, he is at the mercy of others to pick his fallen coin from the ground because he cannot bend so easily. Hence, a tall man has to bend at some particular point of time. He has to bend; I may not reach to his level but he has to come to my level otherwise he will get hurt and may look miserable. Hence, what is the moral? He need not be egoistic that he is tall. When we look at the roads, they have curves and many bends. When we check the water or sewage pipes, they are not straight, when we look at the iron rods used for construction of buildings; they are flexible and bendable, if not the building will collapse. To be psychologically or physically well, one should bend and should be flexible to the society. If this principle is followed by all of us in this society, no one would get hurt or injured. The art of bending and flexing can turn our nation in to a true *Rama Rajya.*

PROBLEM

One day, my friend and I went for a stroll. It so happened that in the midst of the conversation he expressed his problem, which was easily solvable through a minor suggestion. All of us are scared to have any kinds of problem. But still, I feel that it is a beautiful word that cannot become a problem if we try to understand deeply what this problem word stands for; therefore, let us try to know. If we divide this word problem on a hypothetical splitting ground, we notice that this problem has "Emblem which is on probation." This emblem mentioned here is available for a change in that probationary period. If this is true, then how can this problem be a problem? Many readers get confused; let me explain this principle philosophically in a little detailed manner. Say, a described problem in our life exists as an emblem. To give a simple example for this above statement, consider *Ashoka* emblem. This emblem which exists now has gone through the probationary period from *Ashoka 1. Ashoka* emblem has not come just like that, it has a type, a structure and got moulded under hammer before that emblem became true *Ashoka* emblem from *Ashoka 1.* This is what I mean by the problem under probation; if someone understands and moulds the problem, that problem cannot become a problem. Government job initially is under probation, which is modifiable. If a person in a government job does well in the probationary period, he will be taken up permanently;

if he does not do well in this period, he will be thrown out permanently from the government post. Looking at the problem, if we try to understand the problem calmly with great attention and concentration, definitely it can be addressed and solved. A problem in this world exists only to be modified. Hence, problem is not a problem in spiritual *(Vedanthic)* sense. Therefore, people should not brood over a problem. If the problem is taken in the right spirit, the word problem will have no role in our life.

EXAMINATION

A student came to me with a history of fear for her examinations. If we are careful enough to look at the word examination and divide this word by a hypothetical divisionary technique, *Exa* is exit, *Mi* is mission and *Nation* is emotion. Therefore, examination is "Exit from the mission which has emotion (expression of motion)." Generally, any stress or difficulty in our life is an examination. It is true even with every student at school or at college. Life is always dynamic, which keeps moving. Man in this world cannot escape from the ups and downs. It is like a steeple race in modern Olympics. To win, one has to jump thorns, run over sand, get wet in water and climb walls. Hence, man should know that all difficulties in our journey of life are temporary, which keeps coming on and often, so what have we to do? We simply have to get out from such difficulties with simple solutions. These solutions surface visibly only when we are calm. This is exactly what happens in cinema theatre where if we are careful in looking at the signboards of a theatre, we find an 'in' board through which we enter the cinema hall and another 'exit' board through which we come out. Hence, the examination should be like a cinema hall where a movie is screened. Students should perceive the examination as film *Maya Bazar* (a famous south Indian Telugu language movie) but not like *Kolaku Bazar* (garbage market). A student who comes out of the examination hall should be like a happy student who comes out from a cinema hall. We should enjoy the examination just like people enjoy a movie. The students should read their textbooks as any other person who enjoys reading interesting good novels. Anxiety rues the performance. If we are too anxious and have a pre-determined goal of achieving high, then it is detrimental, which lands such students in trouble. Students should know that with little anxiety, he can fare better in his examination; with too much anxiety, he fares badly in his examination. The effort by the candidate is a must or a total necessity; with no effort, the student cannot achieve anything. I had a student who wrote the examination answer sheets with only the name of Lord Ayyappa (famous south Indian deity). Should we think he would pass? His life became *Ayyo Ayyo Appa* (a cry of agony). When we check with a student who has come first, he would not have aspired for the big goal, and also he would not be an extraordinary student; his asset was just a 'no anxiety' state.

INDOOR OR OUTDOOR

The other day it rained. Since our tennis courts were made of clay, tennis could not be played the next morning due to wet court conditions. Among my tennis-playing mates, there was a discussion about the comfort of using a walker at a gym or at home by the rich and the famous. However, for an ordinary man who cannot afford any walker, walking alone on the road side is lovable and most enjoyable.

I enjoy nature; I roam around the city and keep trying new corners and crossroads. On my way, I see big bungalows on either side of the road, dogs behind the gates and the owners behind those dogs with their big moustaches. When I look at his big house, he flexes his muscles in return; by his body language, I imagine that he wants to convey that he has constructed his house better than mine. It is natural that his house is from hard-earned money; hence, no one dares to stare at his house. Many rich and famous, dons and celebrities construct their house with their ill-earned money and not with hard-earned money (not always). A house constructed by hard-earned money has value but not those houses built with money earned through greed. That is why a hut looks at its best when compared to a bungalow. I found that their prestige has over-raided their ignorance. There are small houses and big houses, including huts in the middle, where cattle are reared in front of their huts emitting the fragrance of dung all over. The women are sweeping and the children are playing in front of their small houses or huts; I really enjoy the scenery. These things we do not get to see while walking on a walker at home or at a gym. I know a rich man who takes a walk every day in the slums and nearby places, and he means much for the poor. He spends a lot of money on them and has raised many schools, provided water for these slums, constructed small houses for the needy and given them many health facilities. Hence, people remember him forever. He once made a comment on other rich men, "what is the use of owning five hundred-crore mansion without doing anything in the world for the poor." Yes, this is something to think over, because five hundred crores worth spacious mansion cannot be equated with an ant mole or beehive. Natural is natural; a hut is natural, whereas wealthy bungalows are colourful. A hut has its own natural fragrance. In many depressed patients who come to me, their main complaint is that they 'feel like running away from my home' or a sort of choking sensation when they are inside their homes. In exactly a similar fashion, people do encounter a feeling of lump in their throats when they use such a five hundred-crore worth house or walkers at their homes.

At home, we are straightforward but not so when we are outside. We bend for those who bend to us; it is reciprocation, and we feel happy doing so. The happiness thus produced would prevail throughout the day and that can do wonders for us as well as for others. I cannot sit at home in the morning. I have to play daily, which makes me fresh for the day.

RAZOR OR RAGE

People are proud of their cars. We can touch a car's owner; we cannot touch the owner's car. They are so possessive. I remember my uncle who had a car, Fiat 1978 model, Premier *Padmini*; he would not allow us to sit inside; we all were totally outcast by my uncle. We were 'untouchables'; he was not allowing even his father-in-law to sit inside his car. That was the level of possessiveness he had. He was looking after the car better than his children. I was wondering about this strange phenomenon. Yes, it flashed a moment ago. It looks absurd; in reality it bears the truth. The reader may find interest in my narration.

We have many servants, but one particular servant might not be trusted in spite of all the help we render to him with money or material. This servant feels that whatever we have done to this man is little or nil. He is not contended and he can leak all our secrets, whereas the car is diametrically opposite to his nature. A car has no life and actually is a very faithful servant, a car would never say no and our car takes us to any place wherever we want to go. What the car requires is only our driving sense and navigational technique or proper use of car steering and control on the accelerator. Fuel is cheaper when compared to a living servant. Therefore, we submit our good heart to our car but not even to our wives. We keep quiet even when there is a small injury to our body because small injuries get healed by default and the doctor who attends to the small injury charges only a small fee when compared to any dent to a car. The dent to the car makes us disturbed and depressed because repairing it is expensive; the expense may be alright, but meanwhile, we have to leave the dented car to a mechanic for three days and in those three days; we cannot visit our favourite destinations. The car is an addiction; hence, we all develop withdrawal phenomenon when our car is out of our sight. Therefore, our heart is for our car and if anything happens to our car, we are ready to murder the person who dented our car or bounced on our car. This is exactly what happens during road rage.

Selling the car or any sort of hurt (dent) to the car leads us to grief. What is the moral part of this explanation? Should we really be attached to these cars and land up with dangerous problems? Why should we all not have the same sort of attachment to ourselves, our wives and other fellow beings? Why only for cars? It has to be debated and counter debated in our consciousness. Before we consciously debate, I have something to explain. The humans have veins and arteries, which are God-given gifts. This vascular system in humans has innate fighting and repairing quality. This system in humans contains T-Cells, WBC's, fibrin and other components, which are necessary for repairing after fighting with the micro-alien invasions. Therefore, any invasion by an alien from outside, a scratch or an injury to human body is easily managed by the God-given particles. For this, one need not go to a doctor, and even if he goes, as I have already said, the doctors' fees are cheaper when compared to a tinkerer and a painter. All human beings have a heart; so also, the objects of possession like cars have a hypothetical heart. This car-heart lacks veins, arteries and other materials, which have the power to repair the self.

Therefore, the possessor of this car has two hearts, one is his own heart and another, the hypothetical car's heart, which he owns, because the car that he possesses never utters a single word and his car is totally faithful to him. A car is better than a dog; a dog is always faithful to the master, but at times if this master is not faithful to his wife, his dog might bark at him. A car will never do this; a car just follows the master. As car is so faithful to its master that the master cannot tolerate any scratch, dent or a touch by another car to his car. If this happens or in this situation, the possessor is the loser, he loses his one hypothetical car's heart and so also his money, because repairing his car is very expensive. A car is a mere spectator whether it gets injured or not, but the possessor's ego gets disturbed after losing one's heart in an accident-like situation. This disturbance leads to odd behaviour and in turn this odd behaviour leads to a rage. Both are the losers, the possessor loses his temper and, in this commotion of mind, the victim might get injured or, at its peak, the victim may die. Hence, in this situation, the winner is the car, because car does not know about losing or winning. Therefore, road rage is a rage as well as a razor.

SEX, RELIGION AND INTELLIGENCE

After playing tennis, it is usual to have a customary talk with my tennis-playing mates. Many a times, I land up with problems discussing sex, religion and intelligence. Sometimes, I make bold statements like 'intelligence divides the country whereas common minimal intelligence unites the country.' However, my tennis-playing mates do not accept my statement easily because of their sheer intelligence. It is like yogis who often explain, 'I' we divide but 'we' we unite. Exactly in a similar fashion, intelligence stands for our ego, and thus all the problems begin there. I felt I was very intelligent among my tennis-playing mates; duly, I landed up with many problems. Of late, I have found the easiest and best solution for this problem. The solution is to hold up these three, 'intelligence, sex and religion,' within the four walls of my house, and in any case, I should not bring these three enemies outside my house unless otherwise they are called for. When we watch the spokespersons of either political party in 24/7 TV programs, all are very intelligent, and they keep bombarding their arrows and firing expensive cannon guns that never reach a common point. This egoistic attitude pushes the ordinary man of our country to a state of helplessness. When a common point is not reached, the sufferer is the ordinary men of our country. Any dialogue should culminate with some solution. This never happens in our democracy because all of us are intelligent; hence, we have failed in our country's progress as well as in reaching the poor man. I have seen a person who is filled with "this is my country (*Swabhiman*)" feeling. This man is from a spiritual background. He came to power by shouting the names of many gods and goddesses, and after winning, he became utterly corrupt and amassed lots of money. If this is the true picture of our country, then to whom we can trust or who is going to build our nation?

RESIST NOT EVIL

"Resist not evil," it is a common preaching by many spiritual people of our times. This statement is very confusing for an ordinary man to understand. It has a double meaning in it and either way it is dangerous to society. Observe carefully what it has to say. We keep evil in our mind, resist good things and become a marauder or criminal. We store all good things in our minds and resist only the evil, which is also dangerous to the society. This is what happened with Mahatma Gandhi, who was killed ultimately. Many unseen and unheard of good *Mahathmas* go unrecognised and vanish in thin air. Therefore, have a mix of good and bad. If no evil is in our mind, how can we experience this evil? If we want to be a little enjoyable, we should know the evil within us. Before we drop the evil, we should know the problems the evil creates in us and hardship we experience from this evil. I will explain a few, "If you want to be a big man, you should burn your fingers. If you do not burn, you remain small; burn your fingers and become big." If a reader asks me, how is this possible? I have an answer for him.

"Burning causes injury and agony. Burning is always very painful. You take a lot of precaution to get cured and in that milieu you are silent. This silence makes you to realise the mistakes you have committed. In your agony, you watch your mistakes like people watching a movie. There will be a lot of time before your new skin sprouts or granulates to know a change in your mind. If this burn is not from your side, you see causers, perpetrators, abettors and grievers. If you are lucky, you get the justice; it does not matter even if you do not get justice and let your post-depression days be full of happiness, which could be gained only through your forgiveness. Experience the miracle inside you; you think this *Pawada* (miracle) is because of the doctor's care; actually, it is the 'time' or the *Samyama* (patience). Meanwhile, you should not forget your doctor. This is how a man would grow tall and big. Now you are more aware not to do the same mistake in future when the cause for your present burn is from your side."

Few officials colluding with part-time *Netha's* burn the forest every summer. The reason would be that hunting is easier and valuable trees look better. In this way, they grow tall and taller by wealth but grow smaller and smaller by their greed. Therefore, we should experience both; when we use our discriminative power to wipe out the evil, we might tend to find happiness *(Ananda)*. We should not aspire only for the good or only the bad, we should ask for a mix, which always tastes like a "Fifty-fifty" biscuit.

STUDIOUS VERSUS NON-STUDIOUS

What I narrate now is interesting for those who know a little of *Vedantha.* Many spiritualists have explained *Vedantha;* I will not go into all the details of *Vedantha.* In simple terms, it is the study of manuscripts at infinity. We all know that all of us are identified with name and form. This is equal to 'I' phenomenon, which is necessary for the world to identify the individuals; otherwise, we are not identified. An identified man by nature does not keep quiet. He chooses two types of journeys, one outward journey for his enjoyments and another inward journey for his happiness. Both are required for his self-esteem enhancement. There is a crossover period during which time a man should use his knowledge of *Vedantha* effectively to be called as human. This is possible with renunciation through a way of boundary desiccation between *Purusha* and *Prakruthi.* This arduous journey is possible only through a slight U-turn of a seeker. If a man waits for this bend in his life, which when he uses this bend effectively, that person would leave his footsteps on this earth for others to remember. This is what I call as the eternity. This "We" from "I" is very significant in a man's life. "We" becomes insignificant for a man if he does not pursue to obtain knowledge. This is exactly the essence of life, to become eternal or immortal by an individual. This is what *Sankya* philosophy says, which *Pathanjali* explained through his yoga *Suthras.* I have seen in few service-oriented organisations that the members only keep exchanging badges and mementos between themselves, doing very little service to the society.

Many of us think we are superior with high intelligence. Who am I to think so? Is there are any superior species with superior intelligence in this universe to endorse that we are all-intelligent? We have to wait till that time to call ourselves superiors. I keep telling my clients who come to me with the inferiority complex of not being like other students, "Each one of us is an intelligent and also a dullard." For example, a studious ward is below in his intelligence by not helping his parents. On the other hand, a dull ward is above his intelligence in helping his parents. Therefore, we keep hovering between these two extremities except in some gross psychiatric conditions, such as mental retardation.

One should be very careful in labelling someone, because this label may become permanent. When I say 'mental retardation,' they are the real yogis; it is a God-given gift. We are all bogies and pseudo-yogis. Mentally retarded are true yogis in a sense that they have no attachments. They are totally indifferent to all worldly luxuries except ordeal to their parents. An enlightened master said, "God is there in empty," emptiness is valued most; hence God is with them but not with us. If someone says God is within him, he is a *Dongi* or a conman and deserves what he should deserve under law. Therefore, if we love God or want to find God, we should find Him with such people. A cheater is always intelligent and is dangerous to society; a sub-intelligent man cannot become a conman, so he is good to the society. Choose what you want to be. I remember my friend telling me a proverb in Kannada, *'Mathu Belli, Mouna Bangara.*" That is to say, talking is silver, keeping silent is gold. There is a Shakespeare verse also, "speech is silver and silence is golden."

ROYAL BEGGING

We are all royal beggars; all of us go temples to beg for wealth, health, material possession and position. Do we see people begging for our Mother Nature? We systematically ruin Mother Nature so also our natural ecological system. There is no difference between ordinary beggars and a rich beggar. The common factor is begging, the former begs for food and the latter begs for wealth. Then what can anyone do? We cannot do anything! Definitely, we can do something because something is better than nothing; not everything but only a part of it. This I can do up to 5%, and a rich can do up to 50%. It is left to each individual's discretion. Begging God does not help, it is only his slight illumination or *Gnanodhaya* that helps.

Read this story—I have seen a family, which has four female children. All are adults and ready for marriage. The father never takes interest in finding a groom. His wife has to do everything for the family. As a psychiatrist, I tried my best for a change in him, at least by 1%. That never happened, and I failed. One day, his wife came to me running, panting and was found to be happy. She said there was a U-turn, a *Pawada* (miracle) had happened to her husband. I asked her about the *Pawada.* She said, "Doctor, He is now inquiring about his daughters." There is a strong reason for her happiness because till that time he was completely immersed in alcohol consumption and smoking, and never had his daughter's existence in his mind. A small *Gnanodaya* is sufficient for a man to have a total U-turn. He got his daughters married thereafter. Therefore, in our life, it is just a change or a little bend that is required for happy living. People should not lose hope. The patience of a person can find an answer in this present confused world. One of these days, we all will get *Gnanodaya* for a better tomorrow.

I have another story. A father is worried about his son who refuses to go to school. The father visited all temples and many doctors. In spite of that, he could not get proper treatment for his son and God did not heed to his woes. He was a frustrated and depressed man when he looked at other boys in his son's age. The punitive methods and suitable rewards did not help the boy. One fine morning, his son asked his father as to in which direction the school was situated. The father got excited, kept dancing and told his wife that he had made a fortune; in his happiness, he went around distributing sweets. People were astonished about his behaviour and one of his friends stopped him, and enquired the reason for his ecstasy. He said, "Look, till now, my son's brain was void of any schooling and now he has decided to have a glimpse of schooling." From that day, the father was confident of his son. Later, he became a famous doctor. Therefore, in life, it is only a glimpse or a small ray of light that is required and that light illuminates the darkness inside the man to become a famous man. For this phenomenon to happen we have to wait in our lives, one should not be in a hurry. We should go on a meditative way or the Buddha way.

WHERE IS LORD THIMMAPPA?

One day Lord *Thimmappa* vanished from the *Thirumala.* He had an experience to tell. Once he consulted his psychiatrist, "Look doctor, I am fed up with my place, always noisy and all ill and horrible things keep happening around my place. I want to go out from this place to seek peace, kindly advise me." The psychiatrist got amused and as he had been practicing only in cities, he himself did not know any place where peace was available. What advice a psychiatrist could give in this situation? The psychiatrist said, "Look dear friend, I will go online and search the search engines for places, where on staying there could bring some peace to you." This psychiatrist began searching and kept on enquiring with his friends, but actually, he could not find any place on this earth where Lord *Thimmappa* could hide and get peace. The psychiatrist is always perceived as semi-intelligent by so-called intelligent men; psychiatrists have great ideas in spite of their dull nature. One day, for this psychiatrist, an idea flashed like a bolt from the sky. He immediately rushed to Lord and explained his idea. "See Lord Thimmappa, there is only one place where you can hide very comfortably. That place is a new-born baby because that baby is always pure, uncontaminated and you can stay there only for few hours. As soon as the baby opens his or her eyes, the infant gets attached to this worldly Maya, once again the ordeal for you continues as the baby gets contaminated. So you have to keep on jumping forever between newly born babies in this world." The Lord was very much pleased with the psychiatrist's advice. He rewarded the psychiatrist duly. From that day, Lord *Thimmappa* kept on hiding and his disciples kept on seeing his Stone Idol. This is exactly the reason why we all love our babies.

There is no place on earth that is not contaminated. Air is contaminated, water is contaminated, food is contaminated, an individual is contaminated, forest is contaminated and animals are invading cities due to lack of water and fodder in the forests. At the same time, man is invading the forest for his enjoyment. Therefore, the only place in this world to be at peace is as a new-born baby, just born from the organic Pandora's Box or nature protected mystic organic box of mother's uterus. Therefore, God is not someone who is available easily. God is one who is in our heart as well as in others' heart. Hence, we have to search for Him. The process of searching the God is called as Meditation; working on that meditation is called as '*Samadhi* (contemplation).' If you reach this state of knowledge *(Gnana),* we are liberated to a little extent. This has been taught all over the world by the *Pathanjali* through his Yoga *Suthras.*

Who is this Pathanjali? What does he mean? We do not know his existence, but he is a saint known as Govind Bhatt, who wrote sutras in Sanskrit. These dossiers are very well acknowledged in the field of yoga. Everyone knows what yoga is. It means just a mix between him and the unseen universe or the God. It means so many things for the reader depending on his knowledge and experience. I have a simple formula to explain. Many fights or quarrels in our daily life are because of pre-judgment. No one has time to go in to the depth to find the truth. To purchase time *(Samyama)* and finding the reason for this misunderstanding is called as Yoga. Today, yoga is being commercialised and it was known as three components, they are *Pranayama, Yogasana* and *Meditation.* In other words, the same has been termed as breathing exercise, body exercise and stone-like sitting. It has been commercialised by modern *Gurus,* making a fast buck. A real Yogi never teaches these things but teaches life in general. To know and understand real Yoga, these three explained parts are just prerequisites. Yoga has eight limbs or *"Asta Anga"* or eight parts. If someone is lucky, he would have acquired all these qualities instantly and become the Buddha or Swami Vivekananda. As everyone is not Buddha or Swamy Vivekananda, all of us want to imbibe their persona. This is possible only when we start from basics and this process of achievement requires great attention, concentration, sacrifice and effort. At some time, this energetic ordeal is not at all necessary, and immediately one can achieve things by dropping our entire ego in front of the creator.

CELEBRITY SYNDROME

My friend once asked me, "Why do many celebrities vanish so fast, they disappear, dissipate and meet horrible ends?" What answer can I give him? People have beautiful stories about them. People call such phenomenon as celebrity bash; in psychiatry, the same condition is called as celebrity syndrome. We do not have a fixed definite definition for this peculiar condition wherein each celebrity is different. Whatever may be his strength, he has one thing in common. That is, he cannot live on the moon or mars; he has to stay in this world. Our nature is an excellent preceptor that watches everything, and also whatever is happening around the celebrities. If I say Mother Nature has ears and eyes, people mock and laugh at me. They wonder how? Without life, how can earth watch us or hear us? Yes, definitely it does not have sensing apparatus, but earth or nature is an excellent special living being who keeps watching all of us. Elders would say, "Wall has brass ears and these ears have the capacity to hear whatever we utter or talk, people should be careful before speaking." Generally, celebrities think they have super powers. This unusual thought of power makes the celebrity to attach more to worldly *Maya*. Universe is made up of many planes or departments, which works like CID or KGB. Power of feeling big would allow nature to dig our own graves. Nature will not keep quiet. What it wants from us is submissiveness. However big may be the man, nature takes revenge in many ways. Nature attacks men and women depending on their weakness. All powerful people on earth have their weakness. This weakness is more than sufficient for his or her downward journey. These powerful people do not keep their weakness at check; hence, they succumb to sharp attacks by Nature and perish fast. If they do not understand their weakness and do not realise their self, then they keep on getting attacked. Therefore, they reach their end very fast. This is what happened with Bruce Lee, Michael Jackson, Hitler, etc. By way of inward understanding and realisation, or by way of slight U-turn or bend, the sadness becomes happiness. Then Nature would forgive them, and She would allow these powerful people to survive with more expectations, which they could accomplish for fellow living and non-living beings in many ways. Nature expects each and every one of us to do something for her. She will be happy even if we do not do anything but She does not like people harming Her. I appeal to the people of my country to enrol for the party "not to trouble others." It is a good party for long survival and this party does not allow us to make money. Wealth comes only by troubling others. So, now, one can understand why the rich, famous and powerful who do not understand the inside and outside perish fast without a trace.

I have a story. My friend, Mr Medico was posted next to my ward. He was like a beefy Rafael Nadal. He talks, not by mouth, but talks with his muscles. He was very powerful. While working in the hospital, he got obsessed to a good-looking Miss Black beauty, a nurse. All this happened by some sort of chemistry or a sort of non-verbal communication, which only the lovers can understand. With the usual 'yes' and 'no' love story they got married ultimately. After many years, I met one of his friends and enquired about Mr Medico, "how is he?" He explained, "There is a total transformation." I could not understand him immediately but what he meant was that my friend had changed to a woman and his wife had changed to a man. It was just an Oxytocin shift. Hence, the powerful in this earth cannot be powerful forever.

NANO

I keep mentioning 'common,' which is a very important construct in constructing or building activities, not just material building but building character also and indirectly building our nation too. Today, we find simple families in our society comprising the couple with one child. Hardly, we come across joint families. We are all going towards the nano way. Earlier homes were big; now the same home is small and becoming yet smaller. In this very nano family, if there is no common thinking or no proper coordination or synchronisation, what happens to the family? It gets ruined or perished. This holds good even for the nation. Politicians, who talk more, do not even know the basic pulse of nation and are creating large and wider differences between religious factions by which a hypothetical collision could be expected. Few years down the line, this course of collision may give rise to a super volcanic destruction, which allows the religion to grow and the innocent to die.

What is the root cause for all of our miseries? There is no single root cause for our miseries or problems. We do have one common cause for our misery, that is, 'I am right, you are not right' and 'yes, it is me, me only and you are nothing.' This stubborn attitude divides us as south and north poles. Hence, it often leads to only quarrelling and fighting, not coming to a single point. Why does this happen? This happens because "I do not know who I am, I do not know my existence and I do not know what the other person is?" To know the answers for all these above-mentioned questions is called knowledge. This weakness has been taken advantage of by the *Netas* and other influential people, who by their muscle power and money get sanctioned private schools, colleges and universities, all of whom lack the basic knowledge of running these institutions. It is unfortunate that a good teacher might not get sanctioned a school, college or university because he does not possess the basic three qualities of politics, power and money. When we inquire a peddling rickshaw man, he is proudly sending his child to an English convent. The same story is also true with a housemaid. The rickshaw driver is very happy to be in that elite class. Those who fight for the existence of Kannada or regional language are also happy to send their children to English convents. This weakness in us led to the collection of exorbitant donations as well as fees by these English convents; meanwhile, the poor women teachers who teach English would get a paltry salary as pocket money for their *Alankara* (face powder and lipstick).

NATIONAL FLAG

When it rains, I love to take a walk. That day was 13 August. On that day, I met one of my friends to whom I asked him a curious question, "What do you think of our national flag?" He took this as an opportunity to keep on explaining like a politician. He said our country being the biggest democratic country that represents three religions where our flag is a symbol of acceptance, compassion and togetherness of our population to live and function together. It took almost half an hour for my friend to finish his talk. I felt proud of him because what he knows I do not know. My explanation was different from his version. I explained to him about our national flag in my own version. The national flag is made up of three colours; each colour has abundant meaning towards life's origin and its evolutionary socio-psychological progress rather than mere religion, which all of us have in our minds. Now let me consider the colour at the top, saffron; what does saffron stand for? It stands for fire. What does fire do? It creates heat. The middle part of the flag is white in colour. What does white colour stands for? It stands for compassion. Heat without compassion is destructive but heat with compassion is love. Next, lower down is green colour, what does this signify? It signifies nature or land. Therefore, between heat and compassion, if there is any union to take place in humans, it has to be on some sort of platform. That platform is our land. Hence, union takes place between two opposites, living *Purush* and living *Sthree* is only one of these three constructs. The heat produced along with compassion or act of love should take place on a piece of land, not in the air or under water. Therefore, the national flag represents life in general. Politicians have turned the table only to get political mileage to call the national flag representing three religions of our country. Hence, I define my national flag as life provider, mover and caretaker.

BUDDHA ON THE STREET

I see a person every day on my way home from my clinic. A middle-aged man who is absolutely dirty, filthy, has not brushed and has not taken a bath for a long time, not possessing any interaction with the world, lives and sleeps on the road side and wears soiled thick clothes, which are oversized and are collected from the roadsides. His companions are cow dung, garbage and dogs' excreta. He does not mind eating anything tasty or not tasty, never begs or asks for anything and has a peculiar type of walking and sitting. His left hand holds his oversized pant from falling. While sitting, he brings his right hand in front of his eyes and holds his fingers like the way of Buddhists monks do while they sit for their meditation. Watching him for a year, I have not seen him coughing or falling severely sick. For me, it is easy to make the diagnosis as 'schizophrenia.' After observing him, he appeared completely deluded and hallucinating. He talks less and keeps to himself, not disturbing others. Is he not God-like? After observing this man I felt life comes out of dirt, no life from neatness. This God of isolation always stays with another God of dirt and enjoying God's world where we people cannot enter. Now if we treat him, then the entire problem starts. If he improves like us, I am sure that he would get attached to this world of *Maya* with all the associated problems. What is the essence of explaining this story? I do not ask anyone to become schizophrenic, but in this world, there are two types of major mental illnesses, mania and schizophrenia. I prefer silent schizophrenics to talk and maniacs to become calm a little bit. In this process of change, there exists tranquillity. The powerful and muscular *Netas* and *Babus* are maniacs. Because they never shut their mouth and keep on talking whereas an ordinary man is silent like a schizophrenic. Ordinary man never talks to meet his needs. That is why ordinary men are unattended and our politicians do not care. Unfortunately, if a honest ordinary man opens his mouth, he meets an end like a whistle-blower. This is exactly the reason why I call all of us are maniacs and schizophrenics. Yoga has many shadows with marvellous explanations but for me Yoga means to be like no mania; manic should talk less and work more, and to be like no schizophrenia, he should talk a little more and be bold. In this present situation, is it possible? Let us answer it ourselves. In other words, what Yoga means to me is to have a change in our thinking. That is to say from 100% negativity to come down to 95% and from 5% positivity to go up to 10%. If we start visualising what we have not seen in this 5% change, we can do wonders to the society as well as to the world at large. The process of visualising dark and trying to find the light in this darkness towards good is called meditation. Meditation is not merely closing eyes and visualising weird things. Meditation should be done with open eyes. If somebody does meditation by closing eyes, it becomes *Jada Samadi* (stone meditation).

SILENCE IN OLD

Today, the old men and women as such are not cared for by many. After growing old, some find solace in silence. In this silence, we fall back or go back down the memory line to see our life at its natural beauty. Depending on their account *(Karma),* life looks amazing or disgusting. Many have developed the art of travelling inward with suitable answers for their do's and don'ts. For few, their life looks boring and at sometimes it feels wonderful for all their bad and good, respectively. My friend is so rich that he never bothered to look back, which is not necessary for him because he is marching ahead very smoothly. We friends go for a small debate or an argument on some concepts occasionally. My friend is so good at putting his arguments across; always he would win and I would go home to bring up those statements of arguments that keep coming to my mind like a movie dialogue or like obsessive images. My young friend said, "Yes, you are old, all your reflexes are down, old and dissipating because of which you go past where you try to remember mystic world of heaven *(Swarga)* and hell *(Naraka).* Your time is over, your fuel is running out, you have become slow; hence, you talk of renunciation with the book of *Pathanjali* by your side." My thinking does not stop here, so I tell him, "No, at times, young too renounce their worldly pleasures." My friend does not know that old is gold. If an old man has a mind to jump with proactive attitude, definitely he need not look back. Nevertheless, this speed in an old car is all that is worth? I have seen many rich men who aspire for rest. That rest by the old is alright; meanwhile, the vision of service, sharing experience with the young are welcome. This is where knowledge counts and is an asset in an old man's silence; otherwise, small enlightenment is too far for him. Knowledge is not just books; it is intuitive knowledge. Motivation and hard work for an aged man definitely helps to run faster than young, but at the cost of his skeletal system and heart condition. There are many stories to explain this, but I have come across one such illustrative story. Two friends who shared one hermit wanted to reach one destination, "the wealth." One took the rapid river route and reached the destination in a crippled and unbearable health condition but got the wealth in no time with his huge greed. Another took a longer road route and was slow to reach but enjoyed all the hurdles he came across like thorns, mountains, forest and deserts, and was sound and healthy and accumulated the same amount of wealth with little greed. Without greed no one can make money. The greed accumulated should get converted into contentment to give full meaning to life. If someone says, "I am not greedy," he is lying and he is a cheat and one has to be careful with such types of people. One day, both of them met and the slow-moving friend could not believe his fast-moving friends' crippled body.

The slow man took to the profession of teacher, teaching enlightenment and teaching silence. This man became a real *Guru* and rich people wanted to donate money to make him a big *Swamy,* which he never accepted. He knew the Rasputin story, hence his refusal. The old need not be a non-motive form but still he can be in a dynamic form to spread well to society. It is not the sheer exercises that keep old man's skeleton-muscular system strong but it is the good compassionate mind. Buddhists have embodied such powers. I narrate a recent story. In Japan, when nuclear reactor melted down, the old had offered their support to help the young. This sacrifice, is it not renunciation? Is it not gallant work? Consider Mahatma Gandhi, he could have become the prime minister, but he refused. There are innumerable examples of such people in this world. Why should I explain all these things? Let there not be an excuse for the young to view old as "Incompetent, as the old always looks back because he has a failing fuel." I will not agree to this statement made by the young friend of mine.

YOGA

My friend once asked me, "What is Yoga?"; "Yes," I answered him, "Look, there are so many ways of explaining yoga and the definition depends upon one's intelligence, his experience and also his cultural background." The explanation what I am going to explain to him should be simple; otherwise, my friend would get confused. So I took this as an opportunity to tell one of my concepts, which we use in our day-to-day activity. We perform many automatic actions of which we do not take any notice or try to find the meanings to them. One such thing is 'talk,' a construct that we routinely use in our day-to-day life, where this construct is very important in our communication. Show me any person while talking; does he try to know what this 'talk' means to him? Does he observe the source of his 'talk'? If we try to know this construct of 'talk,' we would tend to become a scientist. I explained to my friend, "Yoga is nothing but knowing many unknown things or in simple terms to know what lies behind the construct of talk." People who scientifically study the basis of this talking are the real Yogis, who belong to one or many disciplines. They are anthropologists, philosophers, evolutionists, neuroscientists, linguistic specialists, speech specialists and ENT doctors. This knowledge of talk is not an easy thing to learn; the process of knowing requires long persuasion, one's effort and their patience. The complete study of the basis of talk and mastering the same is called

Samadi (knowledge or contemplation) or in other words super post-graduation. Do ordinary men know what are all the departments or faculties that work and function behind this simple construct, 'talk'? We try to know a little of this but it is beyond any body's imagination to know the whole knowledge of 'talk.' Should I say that this 'talk' is as the construct of communication made up of certain vibratory frequency where ear and mouth play a major role? In humans, this 'talk' works under the cognition of mind and through the expression of his body, hundreds of other faculties work in-between them, which are beyond my mention. I advised this friend to talk, which always has some value and is useful to others. Speech is a god-given gift. This wonderful gift should not be misused. Slowly, our *Neta's* and *Babu's* are misusing this faculty for ignoble goods. The Ramayana and the Mahabharata are the two sacred epics of ancient India, which our politicians quote and get indulged in non-righteous conduct. It is the *Adharma* and not the *Dharma* that they practice (not all).

There are numerous varieties of talk, mainly, eye talks, body talks and smell talks. For an illusionist, his eye talks, for a body builder with six packs, his body talks and for a lusty man, his smell talks. The talk is an art, which I lack; hence, I could not become a *Neta*, but this construct of 'talk' is a wonderful weapon, which can either unite the world or destroy the world. It is like a double-edged knife. The knife can kill a person and as well as cut a piece of bread to the needy. It is a gift the creator has showered on us. Talk of a person is the perfect mirror of his own thoughts. Lord Buddha was questioned by a king, "who are you?" He answered, "I am the perfect mirror of my thoughts." The talk can be a reflector of characters of a person. Conmen too have good mirror but are externally polished and internally shattered. The talk is a gift and it is said, *"Nudithanthe Nede"* a famous Kannada proverb which says "Act to your talk." The talk and behaviour should be congruent and synchronising. If this is not, a split exists. If this split is proved, then the person is termed as schizophrenic. My professor would say, 'I will prove that all of us are suffering from schizophrenia.' Show me which person is 100% congruent between their functions of brain. The thought does not associate with his talk, the will of the person does not cooperate with his work, the feeling is artificial and it does not go hand-in-hand with other functions of the brain. Therefore, a split always exists at any given point of time to any given person in this world. Hence, my professor is right. There is a theory to call a schizophrenic as schizophrenia. If professor calls a person schizophrenic, that person should be schizophrenic. Therefore, all our friends who worked under him are schizophrenics. Only difference I could find was medication.

The 'talk' can become an AK 47 gun. The 'talk' can fire bullets faster than the AK 47. It can be very destructive and also it can be very constructive. Osama is an example for the first instance; Gandhi was an example for the latter. That is why people call thought (talk reflects the thoughts) as locked-up energy. This energy can lead to a chain reaction just like a nuclear fission. Therefore, released energy can destroy and also can construct. The controlled fission is useful to society whereas the uncontrolled fission can destroy the human race. Osama's thoughts were destructive but still he had some good thoughts, around 10%, which are clouded or in the relative darkness. Truly, we do not have absolute darkness; it has some light around 2 to 5 %.

Hence, one should not lose the hope; one should find or see what we could see in this 2 to 5% light and improve on that. The thoughts of Mahatma Gandhi were for mass construction. He could do this by renunciation. It is not difficult for a person to emulate principles of such great people. These great people on earth could achieve from good reasoning after understanding the society and their environment. The same process is also been called Yoga. The yoga is not just breathing exercises with closed eyes. The knowledge comes with open eyes. Closing eyes with stillness means relaxation. I have seen people closing their eyes and losing their self. That is how men of no substance make merry of this weakness and amass money. Should we expect a golden cot for the man who has no attachment? The opposite example for this is Mahatma Gandhi; he lived in a hut and led a simple life. We should not allow our weakness to ride on us. If we have belief in ourselves, we would reach such a state as that of the Mahatma. '*Swamis*' never come for our rescue when we lose our left arm; it is our wives who come for our rescue.

PSYCHIATRIST VERSUS JUDGE

My friend asked me once, what is the difference between a psychiatrist and a judge? Though I felt it funny, I explained him instantly, "Both punish and restrain." Judge asks the police to lock up the accused and then asks for a trial before giving his verdict on that accused but the psychiatrist asks the people to restrain the excited patient down before giving drugs. The judge puts the convict inside the bars where the jailor makes the convict inactive and the psychiatrist puts the patient in a closed chamber where a psychiatrist's nurse makes the patient inactive by neuroleptic drugs. Jail means to knock down a prime facie convict and a closed ward means to knock the excited patient down. From this, one does not find much of a difference in the management of such a situation between a judge and a psychiatrist. Both should not be prejudiced and should have utmost clarity of mind before the process of knocking somebody down. I have come across a doctor who knocks down a neurotic too. Restlessness, agitation and aggressiveness are common in both conditions of depression and psychosis. He considers neurotics as psychotics and puts them on antipsychotics, where these patients suffer for their whole life because of this knocking out phenomenon, just like a prejudiced judge who puts the innocent ward inside a cell. The only difference between a doctor and a judge is that, for a patient approaching another doctor is cheap, which can be managed easily, but for the accused, to meet another higher judge to prove his innocence is so expensive by which all his money saved would be lost. "I had been a rich man before the judgment but I am poor after the judgment in my favour. I am a poor man when I do not get proper judgment in a lower court; so to prove my innocence with the higher courts I have lost all the money, hence I am a proper pauper now." This also holds good for an ordinary middle-class rural man's treatment in hospitals. A person who was a rich man before going to a tertiary hospital is a pauper while getting discharged from that hospital. Today's education is so expensive; education also comes under this group. I keep saying to my clients. "Save your money, not for your luxury, but for your children's education."

VISHWAMITHRA THEORY

All of us are theory masters. We know many theories but we never try to put them into practice. I explained earlier, intelligence divides the nation, hence it is destructive. The theories are actually mere products of diversified intelligentsia. Theory is proprietorship of the intelligentsia. If this logic is correct, Intelligence has the power of destruction like time-based terrorist bombs; it is also true with theories. One of many such theories is *Viswamithra Theory*. What does this theory mean? We have had many doomsday till now wherein all such doomsdays have become hoax days. *Viswamithra* (the *Janaka* of '*Gayathri Japa*' or sage who wrote *Gayathri Mantra*) was a sage who was not a hoax master. He meant what he is. He is a great sage. This greatness was bestowed upon him by many Gods through his persistent *Thapas* or panacea. In this way, he had won the blessings of innumerable Gods by his *Thapas* (austerity). All Gods and Goddess were scared of this sage. His tongue was so sharp that if he uses his *Shapa* (curse) even *Indira* (king of heaven) could not escape. No God was there till then, who escaped *Viswamithra's* tongue. It was like bazooka as well as the cannon gun. If we had used bazooka and cannon guns, what would have happened to this earth? It was only destruction. This sage would have used his destructive cannon balls, then our whole earth would have vanished but *Viswamithra* was not aware that with massive amount of destructive power still the nature would have left a remnant of life for coming *Yuga's to continue life forever.* In *Vedanthic* terminology, this contraction and expansion is called *Kalpa.* This can stop only when no life residue is left on earth. When we perish, even the earth also perishes, including this wonderful universe. This is what *Vishwamithra* theory means. I have my own explanation for this theory.

One should observe something here. The sage was very angry because people are forgetting what is called "Law of Nature" at a fast pace. Against this law, there are unusual things happening in our society, such as the unmarried (singles) are increasing, homosexuality is increasing, bi- and pan-sexuality are increasing, laboratory sperms have been synthesised, synthetic eggs are manufactured, plastic womb has been developed and role-play by either sex are decreasing and also the women are dominating men. Already there exists woman liberation wherein of late men's liberation is taking its shape slowly. Women are becoming more aggressive and, at the same time, man is becoming more submissive. Womb in a living being is called woman; in today's reality, woman is getting converted into a man after surgical means and still bears the child. Hence, he is bearing womb and giving birth to a child. We do not know who actually the biological parent to this child is. The child is at risk and also the child is in a state of confusion to tell the gender of its biological origin (he or she), which is really a challenging subject in this technological world for further research. Presently, natural and statutory laws are fast changing and thus confusion with despondency is increasing with us. In future, we may not find him or her but may find both in one, then that species is uni-species. Just like plants or invertebrates. For their fertilisation, a third medium would be required. We are regressing because then enjoyment what we have is fast vanishing. Hence, we are searching for new methods to have more pleasures. Fiction is becoming reality, in which everything appears upside down. When this upside down change moves beyond a certain limit the sage Viswamithra would not remain as a passive spectator. He would unleash his great power to destroy the world. Presently, this he brings destruction only through natural calamities, not by nuclear bombs. Calamities like super volcano, great tsunami or by a huge asteroid or falling celestial object might even drag us towards a black hole. The Nature becomes more restless because we are destroying her resources for our benefits as well as for our enjoyments. These destructive natural calamities could be a reality, which can happen early if we fail to understand our Nature and also to put a stop to our greed. This is what Viswamithra Theory means to me. Theory is theory but practicality matters for our survival. Let us be more supportive towards natural fragrance rather than the synthetic aroma, because the latter causes migraine.

DEJA VU AND JAMAIS VU

My friend reads a lot of western novels, especially medical novels. He wanted to become a doctor but he could not. Whenever he comes across some medical terms, he clarifies meanings for these words with me. He encountered *Deja vu* and *Jamais vu* words while he was reading a medical novel. He got confused with these words, for which he wanted clarification from me. I explained to him that they are neurological terms, which are described under epileptic disorders. He left after being clarified by me for those medical terms. These medical terminologies kept on bothering me as obsessions, which led to sleepless nights. I tried to find meanings for those terms as well as I began to relate the meanings of these words to our society, mainly pertaining to family. The neurological definitions for these terms are 'familiar' in a non-familiar place and 'non-familiarity' in a familiar place, respectively. I tried to think of these terms and relate about their true nature in our society.

I ask the reader to be a little more attentive to my narration. When we ask a just married girl, she would explain this phenomenon clearly and loudly; at many instances, her story will be heart-touching. Neurological conditions can be managed efficiently with drugs but not this condition, which happens daily in our Indian society and in my opinion this is a universal phenomenon. I think this agonizing problem can be managed or controlled only by our *Sakshi Bhava* (self-witness). House is a house after all, wherever we go.

Only cultural practices, rearing and expectations are different. We get our daughter married where she enters into a common house, there she feels unfamiliar in a seemingly familiar house. Watch this paradox. What is in neurology is also true in real life. This girl is utterly amused by the new standards set, for the new chemistry of people in that house, for the new culture which they practise, for the dos and don'ts, etc. Truly speaking, these girls are left in a lurch. We do not set any standard with means, modes and meridians for the future outcome of these girls. It is our fault, for one simple reason that we are going towards the nano family's structure. Because of this, we do not teach our children the hardship or immunise them against difficulties, because we have only one daughter, occasionally two. A girl is a curse in our society. Our nation stands fourth in the world in female infanticide. Around 80% lack education. Only 20% have college-level education, but this 20% are not educated regarding family life or life in general. It is a lacuna in our educational system that the girls who eventually move to their husband's families are not made aware of the likely problems and also not made aware of the integrative approach of adjusting to them. Only PhD, engineers and doctors do not help the society, it is the life study that should be a part of our school curriculum. Universities do not teach all students PhD in family management and also in local culture. Elders and family members should encourage our government to take up an active role in inducting such an educational system. We do not do this; instead, we listen to their ego stories and in the same time we get prejudiced, which leads to battle zones *(*Ramayana *and* Mahabharata's *Kurukshethra)*. We do not teach the role-play; it is difficult to teach the same to our children because we are not taught by our elders (many young do not listen to their parents); today there are no schools that impart the important moral stories. Unfortunately, today the moral study periods in our school have been removed across the country.

Today, it is women's liberation, not by the application of Natural Law but by creating statutory law according to the whims and fancies of the present day lawmakers. It was necessary because women have been suppressed earlier. Now this scenario is taking a U-turn, where man is suppressed. This has led to imbalance in the society and in the family structure; thus, suffering is increasing accordingly and also the rate of divorces. Here, chemistry gets converted into gas and heat, never to salt. Chemistry acts as araldite for strong, sound social and psychological bondage. Acceptance is at its low by the receiving family, as the girl who comes does not share their chemistry. This leads to the hardship, despondency, fear, insecurity, suicide, etc. The new entrant has to face all these odds, and live fearing the society. Through some unknown connections, still the whole world is connected, sustaining, standing and continuing. After observing a woman, why should we not view her as the wonder of this world? She overcomes female infanticide, grows up and shuns schooling, she is interested to study but made to work at home, attains maturity and she is looked at as a commodity by village folks, gets married off by her parents with the help of all their savings, she has to get adjusted to the new environment, and meanwhile, conceives either by force and many a times through acceptance. If this born child is a female, then there is a fear of forced abortion. Majority of them dare all and allow the child to grow; so once again the saga or the wheel of fate continues. Considering all these constructs, is she not the "first" wonder of this world? She bears all the brunt of an alcoholic, smoking and gambling husband, adamant in-laws and mischievous children, but still she has survived all these odds.

As such, 'life' is a wonderful construct of this world; some unknown force is interacting with all living and non-living things. Today, we have men's liberation organisations. This has propped up due to a total U-turn in gender status. These already have been dealt under Viswamithra Theory. We can come to good terms if we adopt our proper role-play properly. In between the dos and don'ts of life's menu, there is repression and expression. The repressive visit a psychiatrist and expressive become a non-vegetarian goddess. In between this repression and expression, happiness and unhappiness can be found. The sun is always hot and eye opener and moon is cold and compassionate. We have to draw a line between the Sun and the Moon to bring harmony. If this tranquillity is achieved, innumerable questions would have been answered; hence automatically, many problems would get solved. In between these extremities we have misery and ecstasy, fear and calmness, free and bondage but still life rolls on, and our aim is towards genuine living. After considering all this, I will ask a question, is this life not beautiful? Is it boring? Definitely not boring, because wherever there is ugliness, there is beauty, wherever beauty is present, there is ugliness also. In beauty, we should find ugliness and work on that. In ugliness, we should find beauty and meditate on that. By doing this exercise we all learn harmony or peace. I keep telling, defeat is a laborious word to express, if we remove 'de' then what remains is 'feat,' is it not simple and easy to express? Hence, we should make our life simple and easy.

Otherwise, we lose serenity, which becomes a dysfunction in the easiness (disease). In this fashion, one has to look for good in bad and bad in good. Meditate on bad and enjoy on good. My *Mouna Muni* said, "Take time, sit in front of the mirror, do introspection, see your image, cut that image into pieces, throw away bad pieces and reintegrate the good ones. Again look at yourself in the mirror and now your image is refreshed, you feel free and you are easy going, your image starts glowing *(*Mirror Therapy*)*. Enjoy the happiness inside and feel the reintegrated structure outside. In this fashion, throw away the repulsive energy and you have an accepting energy." A change or a bend in our mind is what is required in us to become humane.

THINK TANK

All of us think; why should somebody be thinking? Why should I think? To question someone, I have to think, and also to answer the question, I have to think. Thinking has come by default. You and I should be lucky to possess this domain or faculty. I think because I am a human, if I do not think, then I am an animal. By Natural law, first to emerge is the body or in Sanskrit the same is called as *Sthoola,* in which thinking is also present but it is at the bottom level. Here the body thinking sticks to only law of procreation or basic instincts. If this has persisted, then we would have seen more fights, quarrels and killings, but present society is devoid of all these things. This is because of well-developed creator's gift *Neo-Encephalon* or forebrain.

For the present state of evolved social human being, the creator had struggled for 42 million years. The creator created five basic elements *(Panchabhuthas)* to fight with themselves to produce a beautiful one Nano of life called amino acid. Several amino acids suited themselves to become a single unit called life. As nature demanded, this primitive life mass thus produced was converted into a complex organic life box with consciousness (sense of understanding through awareness) like us. Thereafter it is like evolutionary give and take policy. For example, I smile and you smile. That is how a social animal evolved. When animal-like behaviour was suppressed by the above said new brain, social man evolved. We all should thank the creator and the Mother Nature. Instead, we are destroying Her. There is an imbalance, the nature wanted us to know Her better but we are unable to understand Her, then why should she keep quiet? She is definitely angry and any time she can kill all of us unless we do not wake up and understand ourselves. We should do proper introspection to realise. Life on earth is diversified; hence, we have to love and enjoy different lives and a variety of non-living things. We should be lucky to have 100 years of wonderful living and with two great gifts. One such gift is smiling and the other is thinking.

Thinking cannot be static; thinking is always dynamic. What exists on this earth also keeps changing; it has to change. If we do not change or bend, we all remain abnormal. If the world does not change, for an onlooker, this world looks boring. Likewise, thinking also should change. The child who also thinks converts that thinking into speech in the form of weeping. The child weeps for its insecurity and hunger. The mother takes care of that child's thinking. What about an adult? He also thinks and this thinking is associated with talking or speaking. He speaks to get his needs. He speaks for his pleasure. He is attached to this world or to this amazing *Maya* because of which he is not able to come out of his bondage. He is engrossed with greed; he thinks of accumulating more money and other material aspects. Money and greed are good for his survival and it should not get fixed there. As he grows up in his thinking, he also should change or bend. If man is placed inside a golden cage, he enjoys the gold and never enjoys the freedom. Happiness is what we get from freedom not by bondage. Watch the dog; when we tie down that dog, it barks; but when we set it free, the dog is lovely, giggling and playful. In similar fashion are our thoughts too. Master said, "Do not tie down your thoughts, leave your thinking free and try to dissolve bonded thinking; when you do so you find the true *Ananda* or happiness. Merge your happiness with the world of happiness; if you do so, you are disengaged a little." This is possible with Yoga or by true Yoga. The Yoga is not just breathing exercise, not just physical exercise or not just closing eyes. Process of liberation or freedom can be obtained from practicing *Kriya Yoga.* That is austerity, self-study and merging with the creator.

PEDIGREE

What is pedigree? Is pedigree restricted only to dogs? The same does not fit for humans? My neighbour put such interesting questions. After explaining the meaning of this pedigree to my neighbour, he got satisfied with my answer and I began thinking deeply. When I began analysing this term pedigree, I felt it a little absurd and funny. When we purchase a dog, we look into its *Karma* or genes before purchasing. What is wrong in choosing the same with a man or a woman? I do not mean the 'purchasing' materially. When we look into 'fall in love' phenomenon, what do they see? They do not see their pedigree but they blindly fall for their chemistry. Chemistry works for their sexual appetite partially whereas pedigree is a process of searching for good genes, which is laborious and expensive too. This process of choosing and searching is actually cumbersome to parents. The present-day love by the young is the shortest route possible to be one of many routes—with bruises to the mind as well as to the body. Responsible parents search for a good family, find their cultural background; look into their educational status, etc. Who decides on this? Is it parents or their wards? With all these odds presently, love marriages are increasing so also divorces. People around them add *Masala* to make the event into a miserable drama with pyrotechnic scenes. Have we taught responsibility to our children and have they thought of responsibility of choosing? For such events, organisations like NGO's, police, politicians and lawmakers add fuel to the already burning fire where they make it glow more. Life is not a movie. Movie ends with marriage, which is a happy ending for the viewers, whereas for the married couple, marriage is a hell. Let this suffering not last for too long but let there exist a bend or U-turn to reconcile from which somehow life rolls on. Today's institute of marriage, the match making is not through love, it is more of a business. This might be the one of many possible reasons for the young to fall in such 'love making.' In such hurried 'love making,' few end up with sorrow in the form of flesh trade, divorce, homicide or suicide. To prevent this drama requires not just an education but a good pedigree.

PERSONALITY

After a set or two sets of tennis, we friends gather on the corridor discussing those players' personalities who would not have turned up to play on that day. Many theories are drawn and many issues on them were discussed. I am just a spectator and mute listener for all those deliberations that took place. I have only acceptance and no rejection. Yes, personality means 'a person with different personas or masks.' The masks comprising good or bad masks, hurting or helping masks, hate and love masks, etc. with varying degrees. We cannot have the same personality or looks, if we do have, then it is difficult to search our wives. Each one of us is different and for each person (man with masks) the personality differs; each is a good subject for a writer to write his story. Many such personalities have been described in texts. Let us understand it in its simplest form. Basically, it is like a bundle of muscles. We have muscle cell, then they group in coordinated manner and that group of muscle cells becomes a mass of muscle goes by the name deltoid or shoulder muscle. Likewise also is the character. It is a combination of traits, schemas, from which his or her character builds. Repeated performed traits mediated by bio-socio-economic-educational-environmental constructs grouped, regrouped in to our schematic boxes, which in turn are kept in our power house or in our consciousness and thereby expressed as character later. Various expressions of these characters make personality. Good character does not come by default, whereas this good character comes through persistent effort and hard work. Let us try to understand one such personality. "Pessimism" is one of the qualities of a character or one of the various expressions of a personality. This instrumental quality of a personality has a value of negative tagging, and thus represents to a sale of commodity. Say apparel, which is undervalued from its original value, which we encounter during sales of such apparels in a business mall or in a particular shop at a particular time. It is fine, if this is done very frequently; then the cloth shop encounters a loss that ultimately would cause closure. Here also the same principle holds good. Once in a while, negativity is fine whereas if this negative tendency trait keeps escalating, we form a type of schema, for example,

1 - It happens only to me,

2 - I am not worthy,

3 - I am unlucky,

4 - I should not have born,

5 - My efforts are in vain, and so on and so forth.

By having such negative thinking, automatic thoughts steps in. This stepping in phenomenon leads to maladaptation of character with difficulties in adjusting to the society. Hence, personality goes awry; such a type of personality does not come under our control. Pessimism increases with added despondency. Emotions start showing odd behaviour in the form of weakness, restlessness, irritability, agitation, etc. When this is beyond our control, depression rules us. This is what cognitive triad means. This sort of personality allows some change in the chemicals or neurotransmitters inside the brain, for example, in some of the many nerve tracts that control emotion. Thus, this change of chemicals within the brain requires outside chemicals to restore. The chemicals researched and tried in medical trials are called antidepressants, which should be tried under professional care, preferably by a psychiatrist and also one should set fractured cognition restructured or regrouped by way of psychotherapy, counselling or cognitive behavioural therapy. A change that is required from negativity to positivity, or a U-turn or a bend is what is required for all these conditions.

A commonly asked question is, "Doctor, what is negative thinking? How is it converted into positive thinking? Is it for the therapist to change us or is our attitude from negative to positive to be changed, how?" To give a simple example, a middle-aged woman comes to my clinic with the history of one complaint that whenever she tries to think only bad thoughts (greedy thoughts or negative thoughts) come to her mind. She thinks about her friend who resides nearby who has purchased a necklace, which this woman does not possess. It is natural for any person to think that way. Her friend's husband works in a government office and his business is to work for the department with added income in the form of bribes. Such people can afford a necklace whereas this woman's husband who works in a private enterprise cannot get a necklace of that kind to her as his income is only a paltry salary with no bribes. Making her aware and realise, asking her to live with understanding of her husband's income is called positive thinking. Is it not simple to understand? Is it an elaborate process? Nobody can change negative into positive all of a sudden or instantaneously. This process of making aware to somebody requires effort, persuasion, practice and knowledge. Hurdles like walls, thorns and stones are common in our life and no one in this world will welcome us with red carpet. Certain life events by way of stress can lead to breakdowns in someone's life. Those life events may lead to morbid psychiatric symptoms for which psychiatric intervention may be needed for certain people. Converting these hardships to free flow nature of mind is called meditation. Process of converting negative attitude to positive attitude by a person is called meditation and when it is not possible by him that can be obtained through professional or by learned men.

ADORABLE EPILEPTIC GIRL

An epileptic adorable girl who is studying in her middle class from a rural poor family background keeps coming for my F/U (follow up) and it is nice to hear from her, 'may I come in, sir,' and after her F/U prescription she would say, ' thank you, sir.' She asked once a very interesting question to me, "Why the head has the skull like a helmet, and not the other parts of body?" I was amused a little and if she had grown in metro cities from an affluent family, she would have definitely become an actress. I put myself into her shoes to explain to her. She could understand a little bit from what I said. I recollected her question later on. I tried to unravel her interesting question. If our whole body is covered by so-called skull-like bone what would have happened to us? We would have been like armoured vintage soldiers with minimal movements or like soldiers portrayed in some of the fiction movies or mythological movies. If this is trues then a hero would hit the villain by only *'Ditchie's'* and *'Latak's,'* no *'Dishum, Dishum.' Dishum* sounds we keep hearing in our movies during fighting. With this bony armoury, orthopaedic surgeons would have been happy. This is just a fiction at present. This might become true afterwards because all fictions are becoming true later. But, why only head should be covered with skull? Is there any reason for such hard bony cover? Let me explain.

Skull is made up of calcium and connective tissue, which is the powerhouse of an individual. It has housed highly evolved electrically auto-charged neuronal cells in billions and billions with its paths, centres, feeders, production houses, conveying wires, chargers, auto breakers, etc. but all these things are present as a mass, which is a very soft material in nature. This organic mass has protein and high fat. Fat is a buffer and an insulator for the electrically charged neurons and if this fat is less than required amount then there will be a short circuit and this short circuit leads to some form of seizures or abnormal behaviour in that person. That is why this structure is very important and should be covered in a highly secured strong bony case. That is exactly the reason why the creator has provided highly secured strong bony box with policing by all senses situated near to our brain. Hence, it is not that easy for an intruder to intrude. This is alright for human beings and what about our man made atomic power houses in nature? Thermal and nuclear power stations are constructed for our daily electricity consumption. We cannot always relay on hydro-electricity, the reason being manmade planned destruction of nature. These atomic thermal stations have been well secured by guards, they also have thick powerful exterior case, which withstands the high temperature and also with buffer or cooling agents, for example enormous amount of water runs through the uranium-rich cells, which splits its atom every fraction of a second, and in turn produces enormous heat and subsequently heat converts water to steam. This steam is made to run through turbines, which rotates fans at high speed, and that is how power or alternate current is produced. If the water as buffer does not run through nuclear power stations, these stations would melt down. Similarly, if fat as buffer is not present in the brain, man would burn down by many neurological disorders. Hence, a strong case like skull is a must to cover and guard brain structures and also allow its smooth function (individual's power house). Therefore, skull like bony structures is not required for other parts of the body. We should thank the creator for such a wonderful work done for humans to survive for a maximum of 100 years. In *Vedanthic* terminology, for such a gift to man, little service to our Mother Earth can also be called as a type of meditation.

YOU OUGHT TO BE THOROUGH

Sometimes, I ponder on my thoughts. Many have offered varied explanations to provide answers to the various questions that I think of, but what is essential when seeking an answer is 'to be thorough.' We know that continuously being thorough builds a good character. What is thoroughness? It can be answered as thoroughness of one's emotions, actions, motivation, etc. As I have explained earlier, a new-born baby's thoughts, as soon as it has come out from the mother's womb, are always pure. This pure thought persists till the baby opens the eyes and looks at mother wherein it starts seeking comfort. Once the baby starts seeking comforts, baby thoughts get contaminated. Therefore, by default, thoughts are always good. Subsequently, as the baby grows as a child then to an adult, his or her learned thoughts get attached with pleasures or to material world of *Maya* (illusion). Because of this mix, he or she becomes bad a little bit. Now, how to root out these corrupt thoughts? Is it really difficult for a conditioned person to have a U-turn? This bend requires effort, practice and devotion. This bend has been well explained by *Pathanjali* in his *Kriya Yoga.* It is not as easy as it is explained and requires real hard work and smooth approach to get rid of this corrupt nature. Corruption is a construct, a protein that has been in our genes for generations. Scientist should identify this protein and an effort should be made to isolate this protein and then subsequently try gene therapy to get rid of this menace. This procedure costs enormous money if there is any; hence the easiest way is to practise non-corruption. How? Simple, live simple, and be content. Thought as such is not painful. Thought hurts when it is attached to emotion (expression of motion). Emotions are feelings. Hence, negative thought is charged with negative feeling and positive thought is charged with positive feeling; frequent exchange of negative or positive feelings produce different unusual thoughts. For example, to the earlier statement,

Pessimistic thoughts are negative ones, for example, being worrisome.

Obsessive thoughts are negative ones, for example, doubts.

Megalo-manic thoughts are positive, for example, to be a king or to be rich.

These expressive thoughts belong to some psychiatric disorders. Repeated thinking of negatively or positively charged thoughts forms a schema and aggregated schemas produce character, many characters lead to a personality. Negative schemas would lead to automatic thinking. For example,

I am born to suffer.

I am not able to compete.

I am inferior to others.

I am not good enough.

It only happens to me.

It is not worth living.

In a similar fashion, the opposite can happen in positive schema-like megalomaniac attitude with the attendant problems.

Automatic thoughts can lead to defective behaviours like dullness with negative thoughts and far-removed positive thoughts, which can lead to misfortunes because of the arising criminal tendencies. The negativity can turn internally towards self and lead to suicidal tendencies.

Secondly, he or she might develop faulty perceptions leading to many personality problems or psychiatric disorders. To explain this, if a person has negative schema, he would perceive himself that he is ugly (body identity disorders), he feels not fit to face the people, he feels people are watching him, he feels he should avoid people, he shuns going out and confines to himself, which would lead to frank social phobia in him later. At times, these negative schemas would become ruminations then later on to frank obsessions. This obsession can become a tormentor, which tears the person's integrity. When this turns inwards, he develops hopelessness, helplessness and subsequently becomes suicidal.

This has been well explained in one of the dossiers by Pathanjali.

Thatha Prathyayath Chitham Ajnanaha
Jnanaha Chitha Vrithi Nirodhaha
Prathibhath Va Sarvam.

Thatha Prathyaya is thought or image; *Chitham* is in brain; *Ajnanaha* means no knowledge or bad thinking or image; *Jnanaha* is knowledgeable or good thought or image; *Nirodhaha* is avoiding, controlling and transforming; *Vrithi* is what is manifested or exists in nature; *Prathibha* is light, light with knowledge, knowing and enlightenment; *Va* is at this moment, at given time; *Sarvam* is the whole world, which is dark including consciousness, if it gets good light, there appears enlightenment.

Exactly in a similar fashion, cognitive restructuring or cognitive behavioural therapy or *Astanga Yoga* helps while treating the depression.

Many teachers bring their children for counselling and one such teacher asked me, doctor, what is a 'mistake'? I pondered on the answer because it was like "why is the sky blue?" I had no choice but answered some nonsense but he believed because he had to. He nodded his head and left my place. I started wondering what this 'mistake' is. I was obsessed with this question. I arrived at the answer but I may not be correct cent percent. Whatever I know I put down in simple words. Consider the word 'mistake.' When I split this word hypothetically, mistake becomes "misses and takes." Now the person what he want to take is missed by him then that taking becomes his mistake. Therefore, he 'mistook the take,' which became a mistake. Hence, whatever we take, if there is no miss in taking, our take cannot become a mistake. Pathanjali in his dossiers asks his disciple to be always to have a highest level of perception where there is no miss in taking signals. If this is followed by all of us, we are sure that there will not be any mistakes. In future with such no mistakes so many problems would not arise. The problems could be avoided if we practices *Desa Bandha Chithaysa Dharana.*

Desa is object to perceive; *Bandha* is tied down, restrain; *Chithasya* is by mind; *Dharana*is *to* concentrate upon, to fix upon.

Now, by all these explanations, it is observed that there are three faculties of cognition that works. First and the foremost is perception, then its analysis and subsequently the expression of the perceived object. If we refine or cleanse these three faculties, then there should not be any mistake. So, let us try them in our life.

Pure thoughts are always God-like from a metaphysicist's point of view, hence it is omnipresent. Different thoughts are always charged but Gods and Goddesses are not charged. Temples are rich and powerful not because of worshiping God but because of thoughts of those who run these temples. By their cheap thinking and people's weakness, temples have become rich and powerful. It is the art of these people in the temples who induce fear in us, and in turn, they have made temples big and powerful. Thought is backed by energy, otherwise it is locked-up energy that can destroy or construct the world or society. If thoughts are devoid of feelings it can be destructive and if a thought has feeling it can be constructive. It is emotion along with the thought, which can dictate that country. The Hitler's thought with particular negative feeling destroyed a particular race. The Gandhi's thought with particular positive feeling constructed India. Thought can kill a person and can also give a helping hand for the needy. Thinking and sub-atomic particles are not different because both cannot be seen but still they are the most powerful. The unseen matter can be used to destroy as in case of atomic bombs and can also be used for constructive purposes as in generation of power through atomic thermal stations. Therefore, if the energy released by nuclear fission is regulated, it is useful and if not regulated it destroys life. In similar fashion, if our thoughts are well regulated then they are useful for mankind but when they are not regulated, the same thoughts can destroy mankind. It is e=mc^2 (physics), which is responsible for nuclear fission, and in human it is the Ego. By regulating our ego, we can avoid chain reaction, thus healthy mind, body and cosmos.

FEAR

A frequently asked question to a psychiatrist by a layman is "What is fear?" If this question is asked abruptly to a psychiatrist, he would get afraid to answer. The fear might have many explanations. Common symptom for all our problems is fear. It has many domains from perception to its analysis, state of the limbic system and the autonomic nervous system, one's expressional qualities, and so on and so forth. Overall, a common physiological and mental state appears irrespective of whatever may be the cause, whether it is from inside or from outside. Anxiety can manifest in the form of tremors, perspiration, fidgeting, restlessness, palpitation, irritability, confusion, blocking the flow of thoughts, etc. anyway, fear is one of the inherent components of the emotional domain of one's personality. It has dual responses, fight or flight. It is necessary for one's survival. Fear is like two faces of a coin or double-edged knife. Each face is judged by the preamble morality. Fear with morality is good to mankind or to the society, for example a wise man. Fear without morality is dangerous to mankind or to the society, for example a psychopath. Fear and anxiety go hand-in-hand. Less fear less anxiety, and vice versa. They are like railway track and moves along the tracks simultaneously. Minimal fear or less anxiety is a driving force for an individual but maximum fear or more anxiety leads to many psychiatric problems.

People see psychiatrist in a different dimension. One might think that psychiatrist is an unusual person because of his looks. Another might think that a psychiatrist should be super intelligent. But psychiatrist is a worthless man if he has no common sense.

INTELLECTUAL

A commonly asked question to any psychiatrist wherever he goes is that, "Doctor what is meant by intelligence? Who is an intellectual?" I tell them, "Look I am not intelligent." Nevertheless, being a psychiatrist, I have to answer them; otherwise people will think I am useless. I asked the same question to a local officer about a KAS (Karnataka Administrative Service) officer who turned into a *Swamiji.* He said, "Yes doctor, an intellectual should have a good service mind." I asked him, "You mean his intelligence is only for the society but not for his family, A KAS officer got changed to *Swamiji* after throwing his wife out." What sort of intellectuality he possess? There is a saying (proverb) in Kannada *'Manege Mari Urige Upakari,"* like alcoholics. They are good for others but not for their wives. If he has learnt the art of life in general he would not have done this. Today, to call a person as Swami he should perform *Brahma Charya* or celibacy. In his case, he would have been a true *Swamiji* if he had celebrated and maintained the old relationship with his wife and also the same relationship of true love with this world. The celibacy in mind what actually a *Yogi* requires, which we yet to see with our modern *Swamis.*

Another friend who is an engineer said, "If someone is to be regarded as intellectual, he should have a logical thinking." This was a good suggestion! This engineer is working in a company called Logistics. Compliancy to his logic really works for a change in his intellectuality. I narrated him a story. In my native place there is one non-vegetarian goddess. Once in three or four years there will be a big festival that is performed in my hometown with full sacredness and festivity. There is one Brahmin family with intellectuals. Because of their intellectuality, many have left my native town and are staying in metros. One intellectual still stays presently in that big family. The native people take his opinion for the conduct of *Jathra* ceremony. They implicitly follow his instructions like sheep. "Do festival," "yes master." "Offer the Goddess a bison," "yes master." Such is the relation between them. He explains to them, "Look, if your place wants to be prosperous and disease free, offer bison, hen, goats and lambs." What sort of logic is this? In the name of goddess, what are we doing? By killing these innocent animals, to which God are we appeasing? What sort of lesson we are going to teach others? Therefore, with logic and with performance of good holds a key for successful intellectuality.

My friend was talking about his niece who got married to a scientist. He holds a PhD in pharmacy and has many fellowships to his credit but he often drives her to her native place to bring some materials. It is said that to be a great adept, he has to have scientific queries with divine knowledge and philosophical thinking. Here, he has got all these qualities but do not apply in his life. We keep see great scientists who have done a lot to the country but actually they do little to their families, and hence separation. The reasons might be innumerable but they fail to understand the life in general. Hence, this scientific knowledge with PhD in life would do a lot of good to this world. Therefore, only knowledge would not make a person intellectual.

I have a friend who is intelligent. As he is a very intelligent man, he sees others as dull. From his attitude, he could dupe and also exploit his fellow people easily. He does this by financing innocents and exploits them to the maximum. Just like few politicians exploiting the electors. He is selective and he knows from whom he gets maximum benefit. I ask many questions regarding his financial business ways, and for all my questions, he gives beautiful answers, which appear very rational. Rationality is nonsense rather than a good defensive mechanism. I explain him a story, once some Bajarang Dal men took out a procession carrying Sri Rama's idol. In that procession, some miscreants threw a stone and that stone decapitated the idol of Sri Rama. Another man from Sri Rama Sena is watching the procession and calls a Bajarang Dal person and tells him, if our group had the same procession with the same idol, if someone had thrown a stone similarly, Sri Rama idol would have ducked. In this story, see the justification and rationality. Is it not nonsense? In our life, we do a lot of mistakes and we keep justifying them. For a psychiatrist, rationality appears as a good defensive mechanism to teach and apply the same in his practice. For ordinary men, this rationality appears fraud. If rationality is followed with practical application then he is intellectual (Rationality with practicality is intellectuality).

THE KING BHARATHA

In places where red brigade is predominant, it is customary to see the public discussing or arguing on some issues. Have we seen people from these states working in their government offices? No. They spend their whole time outside their offices marching with red flag. Today, they take same type of procession with *AK 47* in their hands. Honest work is the hallmark for the progress of a nation. This earlier scenario has changed in this fast-paced competitive world. One day two friends argued on honesty. Arguments went on for several hours with no conclusion. Looking at this construct honesty, how many honest people have been identified as celebrity? None! They are not even identified and they just disappear in thin air. Now because of media, honest people are identified and being identifying they have reached a celebrity status and in turn learn many bad practices due to their compulsions and obsessions. Identification has always invited problems. Who is there now to remember *Gandhiji? Gandhiji* is remembered only when there is *Dharna* (strike) or during election time. Honesty today has no value and it is no more luring. We have forgotten honest *Bharatha* of our epic script the *Ramayana* but we keep remembering present day sports' personalities who are sex addicts, murderers, indulging in extramarital relationship, indulged in drug trafficking and evading excise duty in turn aspiring for *Bharat Ratna.* Where is equality or equal feeling? This country is being run by the common men who pay their income tax, not by these tax evaders. Therefore, who has to receive *Bharat Ratna?*

TAKING SIDES

My uncle was explaining about intellectuality to me. He was telling that to be an intellectual one should not take sides. He is a retired judge, old timer and he is right because a judge should not be prejudiced but today's scenario is different. Compulsions have made us to take one side or another; otherwise, we might find difficulty in leading our life. There are different communities, many languages, numerous casts and innumerable political parties. We have to adopt to live in such styles for our high profile outlook. If we are not in a habit of taking these sides, we remain as ordinary men with a little money, with no power and also we do not get recognised. Human thrives to be recognised and the entire problem starts after he gets recognised. That is how recognised person gets trapped, from which he cannot come out. In order to get recognised, he has to pay, take sides or should belong to a particular community. At this juncture, he is a hero or don or celebrity. At this stage, he is in the centre of dangerous drama where he loses his individuality. His self is lost for many opportunists' who are waiting at periphery. In this situation he cannot be self-centred, loses his freedom because he is hounded by cameras everywhere. He has to live only with extreme brightness; hence, he spends sleepless nights and thus he succumbs to a frank celebrity syndrome. Such is the case then he has to visit a psychiatrist at one or another time. To avoid visiting the psychiatrist the best way is to get unrecognised. This is not possible because he is already trapped. He cannot escape from his own immoral drama theatre in which if he tries to flee, people at periphery sketch, chase and trace to kill him. Hence, the moral of the story is that to have individuality, we should learn to shine 'oneself,' to avoid side taking, to be helpful and to believe in self. Therefore, by taking sides, individual's individual intellectuality gets buried and is not recognised by his or her own real intellectuality. Intellectual's vanishes into thin air whereas poor intellectuals hold their ground. As I have already explained, the compulsions made intellectual people to take sides or otherwise they are threatened and at times they reach the fate of whistle-blowers who have been threatened when they raise alarm against the mafia, corruption and institutional misdeeds. Hence, what honesty can anyone expect from the people? Those who are honest are hidden, their mouths have been locked or they are under surveillances. Who can fight against justice? Who is intellectual in this country? According to me, intellectual is one who is an ordinary common man, earns each day, eats and sleeps well and does a little to this society whenever he gets the opportunity.

VISION

I have a friend; he lost his sight recently due to high myopia with retinal detachment and attendant glaucoma. To his bad luck, he developed optic atrophy, cataract and corneal opacity all in one go. Imagine a person who had vision until now losing his vision abruptly and it is beyond the imaginations of anybody the gravity of depression my friend had got. I was really amazed to see occasional sadness in him; otherwise he was fine and completely immersed in his spirituality. The paradox is that he has such a fantastic future vision to his life but presently he has no physical vision. Those who have physical vision fail in providing compliance towards their life. He published many books on spirituality and also he is well known in literary circles in our place. Why did I explain this? My friend tells me, "Good vision is the hallmark to be an intellectual." Now, what sort of vision? Is it physical or non-physical? We have some *Netas* and *Babus*, literary people, theosophists, scientists and industrialists who have physical vision but little future vision. The vision what they have is narrow, meant for themselves. Their vision is contaminated with ego and greed. Hardly, we are endowed with good vision for the construction of good society. Vision without ego and greed are the hallmark for an individual to be intellectual.

FAN

Do media provide awareness? Do celebrities impart goodness? Any invention in this world has bad and good effects. The bad is hundred and one but good is only five, as per our epic *Mahabharata.* When these high profile people are questioned by the authority, they all answer in one chorus, "We are showmen" but in reality they forget that they have innumerable number of young fans following them. Fans follow them with disastrous ends. Many stories have come to the limelight but these people do not learn out of these stories. Each one of us have what is called *Athmasakshi* or *Sakshibhava*, which should be used by these men or women before accepting roles of acting, which are suitable or not-suitable for public viewing. They should restrain themselves from acting, if it is not-suitable for public at large. I have a verse on fans,

'Fan is a fan a lazy fan in front of a rotating fan,

Fan is a fan a dirty fan in front of a Khan,

Fan is a fan a good fan in front of his "*Kandhan.*"

From this, we should choose which type of fan we want to be. Hence, every celebrity requires *Athmasakshi* or he is the witness to all his deeds and on that he should self-regulate, just like how we regulate our flow of gas in our kitchen's gas cylinder. Through this regulator, one can implode or explode. Implosion can construct a nation and explosion would destroy the nation. No known national agency can impose any force effectively to control or regulate the public, hence each individual by himself has to manufacture and adopt a good inbuilt regulator.

AYYO AYYO APPA

Our country is a good example for a multi-ethnic, multi-cultural and multi-linguistic society. Because of this amazing diversity, two things can happen. An enthusiast can mix with all and be a good entrepreneur. Another can have fear of mixing with subsequent isolation. It is good to see in this present world marriages taking place between different communities or between different languages. Meanwhile, we are inviting many unseen problems. There is one good example where there can be a communication problem between two languages, which could lead to a practical problem. One day my friend who owns a lorry met with an accident in our neighbouring state. The driver of that lorry had to file a complaint in the nearby police station. Because of language differences, the local police could not follow his language. Somehow, he wanted to convey his complaint, which he could do only through sign language. We usually call lorry as lorry but in Malayalam language people are in the habit of twisting their tongue and drag the words with a long musical tone. Hence, lorry becomes 'looriya.' Finally, the driver filed the complaint and returned back. Why did I take this as an example for my explanation? There is one household deity in our neighbouring state named Lord *'Ayyappa.'* People generally know the head of the world being *'Ayya'* or father. Now this *'Ayyappa'* being head of this world, he has to be a God, nothing less than that. My wife never forgets to visit this deity on every Saturday. She is spiritual but not blind to the spirituality. In the early morning on winter seasons, we see people offering their prayers to this God. They chant in a mass as '*Ayya ayya appa, ayya ayya appa.*' Because of this spiritual chanting, these people will go to a state of total trance. While in the course of their chanting the same chant becomes *Ayyo ayyo appa, ayyo ayyo appa.*' In our Kannada language, '*Ayyo*' means a distress call. This is what exactly happens to common commuters who are residing near or around this temple. They will have no sleep, and high levels of noisy chanting leads to noise pollution. The traffic in front of the temple leads to irritation and the garbage they leave after their prayers stinks. The municipality is blindfolded; the people's representatives are mute spectators. They are incompetent to take any steps. If they take any step then in the next election they face humiliating defeat. Because of this, an ordinary man chants "*Ayyo ayyo ayyo appa*, look Mr Ayyo, what have you done to me." This unknown language has been learnt instantly under a trance. This is what exactly happens in some of the Possession syndromes where a person under possession utters an unheard language. He becomes an instant god who collects money by fooling people around him.

PANIPURI

Once I went to a chat centre. I kept my belongings on a chair next to me. I ordered a cup of tea and wanted to relax a bit. At the same time, a family with two children in their middle school arrived and occupied the empty chairs just opposite to my table. As soon as they arrived, the elder of the two ordered for *Panipuri.* The mother was not interested to her elder son ordering *Panipuri* but the father was quick to respond. He was on his toes like a rocket to get the elder son *Panipuri* immediately. Looking at these scenes, my brain began working. I began remembering my school days. I and my sisters were scared to ask any money from our parents. My father was running a paltry business only to meet both ends. We used to fight to get *Masal Vada* (tasty eatery in south India) and *Masala Mixture.* Many a times I used to lift few *Annas* (cents) to get *Idli, Vada* and *Sambar* but my grandfather was so shrewd in keeping the accounts properly; by evening, I was caught and got thrashed by my father. That was the story of the past and today the world is changing. The present day scenario is totally different, what children ask for we get them immediately without realising the value of getting those things to our children. I remember my son's friend who was an extraordinarily intelligent boy and had mastered Swamy Vivekanankda at his young age. He got pampered by his father because of the knowledge he had possessed. If he asked for a camera his father would get him a professional camera, if he asked for a guitar, his father would get him a professional electric guitar. We saw him lately a little weird. The son would browse the Internet the whole night and sleep all day long. Nobody could question him, if he is questioned, he would talk philosophy. One fine day in the middle of the night, he went for a drag race (wheeling) under the influence of vodka. Later, the father found his bones piercing a tree, his flesh strewn all over with instantaneous non-returnable upward journey. Why do I narrate this story? Yes, are we deficient in guiding our children? Are we really going the western way in caring for our children? Would that lead to a legal mess? Is it a sin to punish children lightly? Is there any problem from national human activists or do we come under the ambit of children rights? Each day we keep hearing new rules or new guidance from Lawmakers and governing bodies. Is there any natural guidance or rule or law by being a father who can use this Law with his children? Yes, this Law of father definitely helps his genetic successors. This works only when father takes proper role of being a father. The father should be a teacher, friend and master to his children. He should be a model to his children; he should be a hero to his children. If father is an effective actor then we can see same the effective and responsible acting from his children.

KRIYA YOGA

In our path towards glory or wisdom, we come across many obstacles. Each obstacle in our life is a natural guide. Guide also could be any one, may be parents, brothers and sisters, friends or a neighbour. In our early days, we require just a proper guidance; later, we have to search for the path of good on our own. In our search, we are able to find one such guide who stays till we acquire good guidance and after these guidelines are met, the guide vanishes. A guide can be found for that first time, to find him again is difficult. He will not come back; hence, one should have an initial extraordinary perception or listening quality. I keep telling students, "The master is there for your rescue till you remain as a student and after your learning is over, you are no more a student and the master just disappears into the woods." This is what has been explained in *Kriya Yoga* of *Pathanjali*. That is *Swadhyaya,* which is one component *of Kriya Yoga.* Master is there for those students who are inquisitive. To reach the wisdom, the student has to question himself. Today, there are no readymade answers available. Nobody tucks food with a silver spoon into a student's mouth. The answer or a spoon of food is hard to get now, which could be obtained when a student adopt these three strategies; they should have patience, good skill and total involvement.

We all are attached to these worldly colours, hence conditioned. It is difficult to decondition ourselves from worldly pleasures. The root cause for our worry and miseries are because of these attachments. It is not easy to come out from these attachments because pleasure rules us; we are not ruling the pleasures. We always work with the chemistry but not actually with our consciousness. To kindle this consciousness our discriminative power is a must. To discriminate or to use *Viveka* is a herculean task. The young mind cannot be tuned so easily, they require over tuned masters. Here master is a transformed teacher who has dropped his ego and learnt kindness. Today our masters are scared to talk or abuse or punish children because students have been tortured, sexually abused and punished indiscriminately causing injuries to their mind and body. Nevertheless, students punished in this way are of a very small percentage hence by and large it is impossible to impart good to the young without a little punishment and a non-vulgar abuse. In the present scenario, taming the young though warrants much of a legal mess it should not prevent from teachers imposing slight punishments to their students. We have to have little stress inoculation or otherwise students go the real western way. The youngsters go astray and berserk, which might lead to a lot of psycho-social problems in the family later. Youngsters are the nation builders and if a nation lacks the young, the GDP growth of that country comes down.

CAR ON A HIGHWAY

My friend knows me for my passion for reading spiritual books. He also knows that I am interested in *Pathanjali.* One day he asked me a question, what is *Yoga?* As I have already mentioned, *Yoga* can be explained in many ways depending on one's experience and knowledge. Suddenly, if someone asks a difficult question, it is difficult to answer. I questioned him, "Look, is there any person who is perfect on this earth?" He said "no." Hence, to be yogic he has to be perfect on this earth, which is next to impossible. Therefore, to understand the Yoga, a person has to learn a little perfectness from non-perfectness. How do people become Yogic? This is possible only through a change, what I mean is through bend or a slight U-turn, from non-perfection to perfection. It is the journey towards understanding of the non-perfectness. Let it start from one percent and end with a maximum fifty percent. We do not expect cent percent. The change has to bring harmony or tranquillity. If this attitude is exercised by any person, he can be called Yogic (inclined to practicing *Yoga*). There are many types of *Yoga. Pathanjali Yoga* is popular in our subcontinent. Who is this *Pathanjali?* I know *Pathanjali* as a teacher who gave *Anjali* or otherwise daily spiritual dose through his dossiers for the *Patha* or highway to attain or reach a little enlightenment (*Nirvana* or *Moksha*) than total. To make it simple, to be like a man of understanding rather than knowing. Therefore, this is like reaching our capital on a highway by our car getting its fuel-tank filled every day. The difference is that, here to fill the tank requires money whereas in *Raja Yoga* it requires no money. The latter requires only acceptance and understanding.

MONKEY DANCE

A friend asked me, "What is *Transdental* meditation?" This question is wrong (any way I am not a professor of spirituality); it should be *Trans-Ascedental* rather than *Transdental.* There is a yogic concept whereby practicing *Pranayama* a person can achieve lightness and this person who is said to have attained lightness can work against the gravity. By this lightness, he would be like a bird momentarily. This technique has been taught by many big *Swamis. Pathanjali* also explains the same by attaining liberation or lightness through *Siddi* (special power). He called this as *Transcendence.* This technique is simple, it can be done by any person but what he requires is that he has to make his mind free. This procedure can be explained in this way also, if a person releases his stress out through learned means this person would attain a state of lightness. The simple meaning to this statement is to have a U-turn. It is not the body one has to make light, but it is his mind. This means *Megha* or the cloud state in the mind, which has no obstruction or like free floating. Everybody likes to be a cloud or a bird. We always descend down because this path does not require energy; otherwise, it is a 'free fall.' For this path, earth's gravity helps but ascendancy always requires huge energy to work against the gravity, like in rockets that require enormous lift from liquid oxygen and hydrogen; ignition of this fuel propels rocket to move upwards. Can we climb a mountain like Hillary or Tensing? Climbing mountain requires lot of energy and persistent practice. A change or a U-turn from descending to ascending in our thoughts, in our feelings and our actions are prerequisites for transcendental or in simple terms transformation of our mind. Television shows telecasts the same where people jump like monkeys or like the comic floaters in front of *Swamis* who claims to have such powers only to fool the viewers.

A SCIENTIST AND A SPIRITUALIST

In my practice, I have observed that if a student is too studious and has lot of bookish knowledge, he finds difficulty in adjusting to this society and the converse is also true. Both qualities are rare. If someone possesses both qualities, he comes up well in this present society. It is for the seeker to search for the object of learning and working relentlessly on that. This makes the student a scientist or a spiritualist. One who searches object outside is called a scientist. One who searches object of interest inside him is called a spiritualist. Earlier these two graduates were opposite, but of late, they are coming together closely. Coming to the midpoint from South and North Pole is called harmony or tranquillity. If a seeker approaches this point, it is really wonderful. Too much scientific attitude or too much spiritualistic attitude is dangerous to this society, but in combination, both work wonders for this present world. Scientific inquiry and Spiritualistic thoughts are a good combination for a person to possess. Both are like *Mahabhavo* (Arjuna's mighty shoulders that never saw defeat) A scientist is always studded with *Ahankara* and a spiritualist with *Nirahankara.* Merging these two domains in one *Athma* would take a man to near perfect though not to hundred percent perfectness.

BUSTING BINDI

After the attack on the World Trade Centre in New York a new cult called *"Bindi Busters"* originated from nowhere in America. Their prime target was to attack those women who put red *Bindhi* on their forehead. Their anger is understandable but the innocents were targeted. Targeting such communities or religious people without knowing what actually this *Bindi* means is a dangerous proposition. This *Bindhi* tradition exists in *Hindu* culture where woman of said culture do not go outside without *Bindhi,* which is applied on their forehead. This is also called as *Kumkum* or *Tilak. Vibuthi* has been applied by saints and *swamis*. Men in some culture do put this *Kumkum*. But today we see *Kumkum* being put by some unusual politicians and also with the rowdy elements. Honestly, I do not know why they apply this *Kumkum* on their forehead. In the case of *Netas* or *Babus,* it is *fine*, but why with these rowdy elements? Their appearance is scary. Young and old watch TV shows which projects horrible scary scenes. *Kumkum* with longs and sickles are deadly and dangerous combinations (better to avoid). Why this *Kumkum* has been liked by woman? Let me explain.

If we have an anatomical sagittal section of the brain near the root of the nose, we find three prominent structures. One is entry point of air to lungs or vault of pharynx or root of the nose. Next is the pituitary gland and then foramina magnum where brain stem ends and the spinal cord start. What they mean in our Hindu Philosophy? Let me explain my view, first, why a saint who does *Raja Yoga* gaze or fixes his both eyes to a central point at the root of the nose? This universe or *Brahmanda* is a mega infinite library. There are no written scriptures available to read everything in this world (known library) but it could be there in this universe, which has stored abundant knowledge and that knowledge we can take only through nostrils continuously. Here there is no hindrance unlike university libraries, which restricts public entering. Hence, a person who practices *Raja Yoga* (meditating) observes the entry of only good information from this mega universe through the central point situated near to the vault of his nose symbolically. Knowledge is taken by the way of energy because universe is housing enormous energy (here energy symbolically means knowledge). This energy is also called *Prana* or Quanta and understanding this *Prana* and following its ethos is called *Yama.* That is the reason why we call this procedure as *Pranayama* and this is prerequisite for a man to get enlightened himself from all bondages. *Pranayama* cannot be a mere breathing exercise. This breathing exercise helps a person's mind to attain the highest level of attention and concentration. In *Pranayama,* the breath provides a lot of oxygen to brain for our pure understanding. Hence *Pranayama* does not provide all; it is just prerequisite to acquire the highest knowledge. How? The answer is simple. As explained earlier, *Prana* symbolically means knowledge. Therefore, nostril is the only organ in our body which has free access to this infinite world of knowledge *(Brahman).* Here the reader should understand that the knowledge does not go to a person through his nostrils but the air what he inhales makes him more attentive and in turn increases his concentration. The extra oxygen what is abundantly available in the atmosphere allows other senses to perform their duties well in him. This is how *Pranayama* helps a person to go up in his thinking. Therefore, the said knowledge or energy has to go to the brain through the nostrils only, not by mouth. The explanation I narrate here is more abstract to say air and knowledge are interlinked and interdependent. Only sick person breathe air from their mouth for want of more oxygen. Air through nostrils increases oxygen level but air through mouth increases alkalosis levels in the blood stream, which in turn leads to the muscle contraction (alkalotic tetany) as we see in some anxiety states. To get more oxygen in such states of anxiety hurried breathing is seen due to the shortness of breath. In psychiatry, this state is called as "Hyper Ventilation Syndrome."

We are all products of our Mother Nature, the mother asks us to use our nostrils to take the knowledge, not by our mouth. If we take knowledge through our mouth, this knowledge goes to our stomach in the form of food. This food should be sufficient to provide required glucose to the brain. If we take extra food, it is dangerous for the body and also to the mind but in the case of Pranayama any amount of air can be inhaled, without restrictions whatsoever. More the oxygen we inhale, more the knowledge we acquire. Brain is the powerhouse to store this knowledge. After storing the excess knowledge in the said powerhouse the seeker can exercise his powers to merge his consciousness with nature's consciousness. This mix just explained is otherwise called Yoga. Hence, one can see the importance of using this *Bindi* or *Kumkum* with women or men alike.

Secondly, along the plane of this *Bindi* we have the most important organ called pituitary gland and this is the mystic gland meant for our feeling (*Bhavana*). Many argue that in this plane lie a mysterious, non-understandable, mythological and also a hypothetical pineal gland, which is said to be absorbing all the knowledge possessed in this environment and in turn this gland emits intuitive thoughts. This gland is also called the third eye. This hypothesis does not give any substantial scientific understanding. It remains as mythological as Shiva's third eye *(Thrayambhaka)*. Any way for common understanding through this pituitary axis, called HPA axis (Hypothalamus Pituitary Adrenal axis), of all our feelings, essence of living and sustenance of our body and as well as our psychological health is controlled by the release of various hormones appropriately and harmoniously to the timely need of a person through various interactive and complementary nervous plexus, its nerve connections and the individual hormone receptors with barriers. This gland in actuality is very important in humans because this pituitary gland secretes Oxytocin hormone, which keeps the whole body united with the world through *Bhavana* (feelings or emotions). Without this, we all would have become demons. You ask me how? Creator by default has given this hormone, which gets secreted in excess during parturition only to get mother hood for her child. This is exactly the essence of this pituitary gland, which is situated in the line of *Bindi.* Many studies have been conducted where this hormone is in excess, produces calmness and caring attitude. Unfortunately in our society because of so many varied reasons like change in to present technical world and transition from orthodoxy to free society, the levels of this *Oxytocin* keeps on changing. Woman till now was suppressed. She was used as a commodity, which led to favourable policies to woman by our government, judiciary, and other nongovernmental organisations. This transitional change led this hormone, which was abundant to redundant, so also in its function. The true womanhood is secondary to the good secretion of Oxytocin levels. When this hormone is at its optimal level, she can be termed as real woman of wisdom with hundred percent caring attitudes. Generally, in this mean society woman's feelings are coming down and also their role-play in the family is automatically getting decreased. She is becoming more independent because of her education, easy job opportunity, increased awareness, independent attitude, equal status and responsibility. This has led to certain psycho-social problems in our society through changed emotions and feeling of her. Division in the feminist attitude led to chaos in family atmospheres. This chaotic atmosphere has diminished the joy of family life. This has made pleasure less, irresponsible attitude, suspicion leading to a paraonidity in few. Trust is lost, smile has become artificial, actions are counter checked, favours to be doubted, and so on and so forth. This has led to a neo change; a different outlook with either sex, extremes of this culminates in divorces. Added to this problem, never-give-up attitude in family has led to mal adjustments. This has created an ostrich egg of ego, which cannot be cracked by us so easily. By the time it is cracked, no help or support would help her or him.

The caring attitude from woman is decreasing but in contrast caring is been increasing with men, a paradox. This is why woman reservation bill till now is not been passed in the parliament, debate is still going on. It is not only the reason why a woman has not given such status. The other hypothetical reason is that, her Oxytocin levels keep getting disturbed more and more by other sex hormones, which have an influence on this hormone. Because of this, woman cannot have harmonised or balanced thinking at any given point of time as her thinking is directly proportional to the optimum levels of Oxytocin. This does not mean that they are totally bad but at their executive skill levels and decision making there could be a little error of judgment. This neuro hormonal interaction should be known by each woman who is at the top post. Exceptions are the rule, there are many women who ruled many countries in a better way when compared to their counter parts but by and large it is not so. In men this will not happen and if there is any influence of hormone on them, that can happen on two times, in puberty and in climacteric stage. Hence, it is said that men's thinking is better when compared to woman but it is not totally true. This is exactly the reason why in one of the major religion members keep their women where they should be. Their religious attitude, atrocity against woman and notorious outlook on them made that religion mean. Intention is OK, but at the same time, the men in that religion should give woman the liberty and humanitarian treatment which they really deserved for. That is how some hate *Bindi* or *Kumkum*. Some attack on these women who have applied *Bindi* because they do not know the symbolic value of central point in the forehead. Oxytocin hormone is known for its compassion and empathy. The festivals, the meet on social occasions or in some religious conglomeration, meeting people and friends enhance the levels of this Oxytocin. True Yoga or practice of any kind of Yoga enhances this hormone levels, which in turn gives the required calmness and compassion to humans. The practice of Yoga is not easy to practice; this requires lot of energy by the individuals. Hence, by default in Hindu culture the *Bindi* or *Kumkum* application at the root of the nose or at the frown of frontal region has come down from generation to generation only to proclaim that, "Look our woman hood has necessary calmness and compassion to take care of the family and the society." It is just like a ritual 'sacred thread ceremony' for males. This is done at certain age or before he getting married in Hindu culture. Once again it has symbolic meaning that is "Look now, I am grown up and acquired knowledge to take care of you as my life partner."

Next and the most important anatomical structure is foramina magnum or *Brahma Randhra*, where brain stem ends and spinal cord starts. Spinal cord is primitive and the new brain (neo encephalon or frontal lobe) evolved made man human and this is a recently developed organ as per the evolution of man is considered. These days, living fraternity is losing humanity fast, and we are losing humbleness because life has become more mechanical and complicated. In the present confused world, we have to search for humility. In humans, this frontal lobe controls the most primitive spinal cord. This *Bindi* or *Kumkum* symbolically represents this spot. Unfortunately, we see this big *Kumkum* on the forehead of bad people. This entry and exit from the brain to spinal cord and vice versa at this junction or the small opening is a super high way for the traffic of millions of signals on either way. From this millions of signals what is perceived through sensory organs go up to the brain to get filtered, processed, assimilated, logically placed, stored, executed with skill and intelligence to live, flee or to face this ever complicated, hurdle ridden and changing world. Therefore, this *Kumkum* or *Bindi* symbolically represents the spot where a gate way to *Moksha* (panacea) exists.

GOD FELLOW

One day my friend asked me, "Have you come across God fellow?" I got confused and I could not answer immediately. I told him that I would answer the same in a day. Coming home and thinking of god is always a tricky business, because God we talk about is omniscient, omnipotent and omnipresent. I asked my wife about God, she said God is only to feel and not to be felt like current. My children would not agree on this explanation because they explain what the current is. I kept on scratching my head and no answer came to my mind. I am definite that I do not have a definition for my friend's God but I have a definition only for my imaginary God. Today, no one is ready to listen to my definition because everyone wants a *Nano* answers like tweeting business. With the tweet some (celebrity) become famous in no time. Tweeting is an art and it is like a multiple choice question, 'yes' or 'no' and for both we get 'likes.' Tweeting is like women wearing clothes, when we tweet short that tweet appears beautiful. When a woman wears more scanty clothes, she appears more beautiful, just like heroines wearing clothes in Hollywood award ceremonies.

God is a beautiful word, and by default, this God is there with all of us. If we are slapped by somebody 'O'-God, if someone get amused or excited 'O'-God, if we get wealth or lose wealth 'O'-God and during orgasm 'O'-God and during calamities also 'O'-God. Somehow or by some means, this whole world is united with this God and also divided by the same God. If we observe carefully this world is divided through religion. In some places, the world is united without this religion and God is the root cause for the entire phenomenon. According to me, we have two types of God spots in us. One is below and another is at top. Much divorce we see today is for the same reason that bodiless husband whose God spot is at top which is in upper chamber and the headless woman whose god spot is below which is in bottom chamber. To bring these two to one spot is difficult and requires a lot of understanding, patience and time. As I have already told, today no one wait, as everything should happen immediately or urgently. Then how can these God spots converge at one place? As couples do not have time to understand this, the incidence of divorce is in an upward trend and the lawyers are making merry of this situation.

Today we do not know about the origin of the universe and our scientists are making their effort to know, but each time they try, they fail. Then how did we exist and what was our origin? If we observe carefully, there are three letters in *GOD,* and we can come to some conclusion. Letter 'G' stands for geologically, letter 'O' stands for orderly and the last letter 'D' stands for developed. Hence, we are geologically orderly developed organisms and because of which we are all god fellows. As per the saint Adi Shankaracharya, who said, 'I Am The Supreme Being, I House My Body And My Mind As Well As *Ago Brahman.'* Therefore, I am *Aham Brhamsmi.* This is *Vedanthic* trilogy. God is within us and we go in search of this God outside. In this search of God, we die in stampedes, we die in accidents and some die out of diseases. We never try to search for God inside.

We spend our time in searching for God outside, which has to be stopped. We have enough number of Gods inside or like *Sankeerna* or mega mall of Gods. To search we have to have a good light. In a mall, we search for good products; similarly we house in our self-good aspects and bad aspects. The art of searching the goodness is called Meditation. One need not close our eyes to meditate but meditation can be done with our eyes open. This type of meditation requires observation like an eagle's eye. Good effort, moderate patience and little practice makes meditation better.

LIVE STOCK OR BANANA

One of my patients did not keep in his pre-appointed date. When enquired regarding his failure to come on the date of appointment, he told me about his visit to a festival in the nearby village, where in the festival, live hens, lambs and goats are thrown over the cart just like people throw banana generally. I wondered and felt sorry for the innocent birds and animals. What sort of festival is this? Some hens die out of fear or the goat's lose their limbs or the sheep's internal organs bulge out in the stampede. Imagine for a goat or for a lamb losing limbs or fracturing ribs. After visualising these scenes, I see animals with pleading eyes, staring at God to show mercy on them and asking God to give advice to the most inhuman humans not to do so. For this sort of brutality, this dirty man requires maximum punishment or conviction. If the lambs and goat had strongly built hands and little brain, they would have been equipped with longs, knives and chains to fight humans. Unfortunately, they do not possess and they are at the mercy of so-called humans who are really idiots and marauders. When I had an argument with one of my friends, he said, 'Yes, God has endowed lambs and goats with no hands and brain. He has endowed canine teeth for us to eat them.' This is the nature of peoples' thinking. What advice can anyone give to such people?

BHADRA KALI OR CHAMUNDI

If we observe carefully in our culture, there is no male God in our country where we offer non-vegetarian food but we always offer vegetarian food to such Gods. We find many female Gods to whom we offer non-vegetarian food. Why is it so that this type of cultural rituals exists in our society only? Many might give many answers but there is one important symbolic meaning in this type of offering. I have my own view to explain these rituals. I leave it to the reader's discretion. When we look at the village woman in our society, she is been confronted with many hurdles and hardships. What does this Goddess *Chamundi* mean? *Mundi* means head of a woman under *Chamara* (umbrella). Under this umbrella, a woman has innumerable works to perform, hence lots of stress and also she has to take care of many household chores. Hence, a woman in our society is always *Hot.* She is like *Mirchi.* However, this hotness is considered by our cultural background through a God-given hormone *Oxytocin.* With this hormone, the *Mirchi* nature of a woman or hotness would be reduced and that is how invariably a woman in our society is calm by default. If this process takes U-turn, then the woman turns into Goddess *Kali* and no one could sustain Her power. We all would perish in no time if she unleashes Her power, which She possesses. Generally, 98 % of our women do not become *Chamundi* or *Kali* in our society but if we take a journey inside our country or into the heart of our country, she is the most beautiful creature on this earth. What all she does? She does everything, takes care of the in-laws, takes care of her husband and children, she does cooking, she gets water from the distant well, she works in the field, she does household works, etc. *Maha Kali* has been endowed with eight hands, which symbolically mean that at any given point of time she is well tuned to work more than one assignment. From time immemorial, because of her special nature, she can work all eight jobs at one go. The explanation what I am giving is all symbolic. I had a junior in my institute who works as a coordinator in an outsourcing company to conduct some drug trials on humans by a drug research company. He has been gifted by God to answer five to six questions at a time. Is it not nature's gift? Actually speaking, I cannot handle two or three questions at any given point of time. I get irritated in this situation but this junior is so compassionate and cool in managing these questions in one going. This is possible only with our village women folks but not by our men. This is true, I have seen same qualities with my wife and hats off to her but I really feel ashamed in front of her because I regret of harassing her and quarrelling with her, but the compassion what she had towards me was something amazing which I could not express. If she was not having the compassion towards me she would have turned to *Kali*. In that case, I would not have been here, probably I would have been on the streets. A woman swallows all her difficulties and still she is the building block of our country. Many men of our villages go towards the town; they spend their time smoking and do many dirty things from morning to evening. They return late to the village. However, a woman does all the work before the arrival of her spouse. Actually, it is more work for her. Therefore, Goddess is non-vegetarian always because she can digest everything on this earth and this is more of symbolical digestion. When we have a look at the *Kali's* tongue, it is red and that means she can taste blood and as well all living beings on this earth. This has some meaning towards the digestion of hard work she does in the villages. However, what do we do? Instead of praising her, we offer Her live lamb, live hen and live goat. We decapitate bison to appease Her, and at times we perform human sacrifices. In this twentieth century, do we require all this? Where are we heading to? Are we going back to our primitive life? If we understand the non-vegetarian goddess deeply, probably this sort of rituals in our culture stops. If we understand our woman properly and give our helping hand to our women, not to the complete extent, but at least a small percent, then many such sacrifices could be stopped. These rituals have taken many forms of lucrative festivals, not caring for the statutory law. Law enforcers have become incompetents to all these ceremonial rituals. Because of political colouring and intellectual interferences this sort of dirty practices have continued relentlessly and also such practices are going to continue in future too.

A TWEETER AND A GREETER

Tweeter is one who tweets through idiot box. What does he tweet? A message consists of a few words or a sentence. It should be from a celebrity or from high profile people; in fact, tweet is supposed to carry a meaning to society in general and also should have some value to build the nation or life. Paradoxically, some tweet with meaning to harm others, to make a comment, to pull the leg of someone, at times having a commodity value or with some personal information, etc. You tweet short and you become famous in the shortest possible time, like a Bollywood actress (scanty clothing). If tweet is not short, tweet appears like a Hollywood actor (full suit and boot). A tweeter is an isolated man and confined to a place where he does not like interferences and believes in social network only (Social Disconnect Syndrome). Greeter is diametrically the opposite and also a type who does not believe in social network but he believes by physical presence sharing no idiot box but he shares people with the spirit. Both purposes are same with larger participation without local presence in first but smaller participation in next with full of interference and at times leading to happy or disastrous ending. After all, man is a social animal and it is his choice to choose, to be a 'tweeter' or a 'greeter.' Greeter has to spend money whereas tweeter need not. Tweeter has to spend only his brain. A tweeter is happy depending on the responses he receives but not the greeter. A greeter is not happy because he spoils his health by drinking alcohol too much and also he spoils his mind by spending his more money which might push him to debt crisis.

A CRITICISER AND A CONSTRUCTOR

There is a good old saying in *Vedantha* 'Known, knower and knowing.' This means that for an object there is a subject, after studying the object by the subject what conclusion the subject has drawn out of the object is called knowing. Knower is all right but this will not do everything in life. If somebody wants to excel or come good in his life, it is not just knowledge but knowing what actually man requires. Knowing always helps to illuminate one's mind. Many have done double degrees and have PhD's to their kitties but in vain. He is a knower but no knowing; hence fails miserably in his life. Knower is always a criticiser; he is intelligent, meanwhile, he is a big hinderer in constructing this world. Where a person who has mastered the art of knowing is not a hinderer, he is a constructor. Hence, master who knows knowing cannot be a hinderer; he goes silent and works relentlessly without asking for anything in return. This is what Buddha did. The person who has qualities of knowing is a brick for the construction of this beautiful world. *Yoga* means to go beyond the knowledge. My friend said, "Dear friend you have everything with you and what is the necessity to read and work?" Is it all what we require? The glimpse with light beyond material, reading and working would do wonder to this world. I explain, "Look, you have been placed by default in one of the major religious group, because of which you are comfortable; no hassles to you and you appear to be more powerful.

Do not look at your own religion for comfort but to be more comfortable you see beyond your religion. Religion is one side of the coin but on the other side of this coin there are other religious groups present. Hence, study and understand those religious groups too. If you understand your religion, you feel you are free but still this liberation is elusive to you. When you accept all religions, you can achieve a little liberation." That is how a person can live with no fear as he would not have any attachments with any religion.

People visit temples and hop around mutts to find the blessing of Gods and *Swamies* for the fear of ill they commit in their life but they forgets that they have God inside them and that is nothing but their own goodness. Off late, all of a sudden, *Bhakthi* has increased with people of either religion. It is not real *Bhakthi* but appears more of a pseudo-*Bhakthi* to me. When we look at the temples, the mosques, and also many churches, we find people in full. Because of these wealthy members, temples and mosques are becoming richer and richer day-by-day but their devotees are becoming poorer and poorer not at monetary level but at their knowledge level. When we see car festivals, people gather in thousands. The same is also true with *Urus;* here also people gather in thousands. Why do they gather in thousands? They gather only for the want of a gathering by either religion. For an onlooker, there is a sea of humans, not to imbibe humanity. There is some catalyst, which has kept these two extremes in check, and if this catalyst exhausts, then there will be a reaction with negative and positive charges, which will lead to neutron or proton bomb explosion. So, this could be prevented by thorough understanding of the real pulp of either religion and not by just visiting respective Gods. This sort of cluster worshiping would lead to disastrous aftereffects; the present-day *Netas* soft appeasement approach actually divides the country. Hence, religiosity as such cannot construct; it can destroy the country. Deep understanding of many religions can construct our beautiful nation. There is only one group in which every citizen of our country should follow and take the oath as 'I am an Indian and I pledge my whole life to work for building my nation, let my children not suffer in future.'

BEE

"I am an employer, I employ an employee and I want the employee to work with honesty to the extent of 100% and being an employer I expect an employee to fall in this line." This is the attitude of all the private corporate establishments. Employer has the ego over his employee for paying for the work rendered by employee and employee has the ego over employer that he is being paid for his hard work. Both fail to understand that their egos are the deterrent factors for their company's further development. It cannot happen now, because pink and red slips are dispersed frequently and employees are scared in IT and BT sectors. It is good to see because our country is prospering at the cost of strain and work load of employees. Here, the employer is the ruler, but at the government level, the employee is the ruler. What a contrast! This has led to many problems like achieving given or expected targets. Whatever said and done, I would like to narrate a story of bee. Bees are the most efficient workers I have come across and observed. When I get up early in the morning before sunrise, through the window, bees get attracted to the light switched on, because there was one beehive on the top of my bathroom window. Bee thinks the light I switched on is the natural sun and this artificial light is true morning for the bee because of which the bee being a workaholic and obsessed with the work cannot differentiate what is artificial light and what is natural light. The bee just zooms inside my window and keeps buzzing haphazardly in search of a flower to suck honey *(Makarandha)* in vain; this bee goes for a trap and gets killed in that sweltering heat the bulb produced. What is the essence? Essence is that its sincerity *(Niste)* towards the lady bee and the innate mechanism to work, not for its sake but for the group. Here bee's vision is only for 'we,' but not for 'I.' If this essence is followed by the employees employed by the governmental institutions, imagine where our country will be heading to. If we want to have a bend or turn from developing to developed country, it is sincerity and working attitude like the bee that is required.

THE HYPNOTISM, THE BOGUS AND THE SOUL

What is hypnotism? It is a common FAQ (frequently asked question) by many people to a psychiatrist wherever he goes. There are many stories and beautiful writings on this hypnotism. There was a time when hypnotism was the only treatment for all mental illnesses. All of a sudden, hypnotists grew in large numbers all over the world and also these hypnotists were rich in no time. As days gone by, the frontier of science did not accept the role of hypnotism in curing all psychological illness to 100% but it is said that it has some role to play as a non-pharmacological or alternate type of management for some neurotic illnesses. Now as hypnotists got richer monetarily and poorer by their knowledge a new school called *Punarjanma* or reincarnation started. Such schools are growing in cities by intelligent cunning and talkative men. For all odd behaviour of people, these men claim is to regress them to their past by hypnotism and explain to them their demonic and horrible life under their trance. Thus, they give rosy reasons for people's odd or neurotic behaviour. If a person behaves like a monkey, they would say that in his past life he was a monkey or *Lord Hanuman.* If he is a rogue, they would explain that he was possessed by a demon in his past life and if he is good man they would say he is the reincarnation of *Rama*, and so on and so forth.

What is the authenticity, what actually science would say? Many theories and research materials are available but they cannot explain this phenomenon objectively. I have my own way of explaining this phenomenon. I may be right or wrong but I just try to explain. Whom does the hypnotist hypnotise? Everyone is of the opinion that a person who is suggestible can be hypnotised. Who are those people? All psychiatric books explain those particular personality traits who are histrionics or suggestible. Who is hysteric? To tell in few words, they are colourful in their approach, highly demanding, shallow with their emotions, having superficial relationships, craving for beauty, attention seekers and aspire to be like a celebrity. These are the persons who provide beautiful explanations of their pasts, which have great *Masala* (pepper, salt, chilli and other synthetic material to taste good) which taste junk. Hypnotist takes them to around hundred to two hundred years past in their deep hypnotic state. How this client could hear the hypnotist's commands when he is in a deep normal sleep? Because when a person is in his normal deep sleep, he cannot hear any voice. To hear, he has to be awake. Therefore, for all practical purpose, he is awake. This sleep state should be authenticated by EEG recordings. Now the client being awake and highly active and also because of being a dramatic person, he listens to all commands by a hypnotist and in turn this client keeps giving *Masala* explanations. We the people believe these pseudo-colourful junk narrations in this world.

What is *Athman* or soul? It is a prime product, which has been capitalised by many modern *Swamis* to amass money to become famous. Poor *Athman* or soul of the ignorant lot of Hinduism has led to confusion wherein said 'self' has been made as a platform by bad intellects to take advantage of innocents. Under this group, religious decency and dignity are being hijacked wherein the wonderful concept of the *Athman* is lost. Why this *Athman* is wonderful? In my view, for those who know soul is like 'Mysore Pak,' and for those who do not know the soul, it is like *Mirchi* (chilly). Soul is a wonderful object, which has no form and name, and it is all pervading. It is beyond science, and hence, omnipotent. It has no smell; hence, omniscient, and it is not present hence omnipresent. Then *Athaman* cannot become anything except God. I have explained earlier what God means. This soul is necessary for the nature to exist. If soul was not there then this nature would also not have been existed. This is like our currency. Without the RBI seal and president's signature on a piece of paper, this paper has no value. So also this soul stamp on nature which is most valued. This Nature has created us and that is how this nature exists.

This *Ago Brahman* or the whole universe is not a separate entity, just like *Aham Brhamasmi.* Nature has innumerable souls which are mixed up but for the nature it is an ardent task or difficult to identify separate souls. Hence there should be a unit to express this wonderful soul for which there should be an expressing case with definite boundary and that casing made is an art by the creator. This casing is made up of complicated organic functional mass with minerals and water. Nature comprising five basic elements fought vigorously for thousands and thousands of years to produce a single amino acid, which comprises oxygen, carbon, hydrogen and nitrogen. This amino acid was intelligent enough to suit the hostile and friendly conditions of this nature. With different formulas, the synthesised amino acids grouped and changed subsequently to a beautiful magnificent ultra-microscopic carbon chip called genes and these genes in succession evolved to physical casing that appears as we today. Organic case has a magical, mystique with ultra-unseen and unfelt functions, which is called consciousness. This product is very subtle (unexplainable) in its existence and functioning. We are all sustaining and functioning by beautiful interaction between this consciousness and wonderful nature. Hence, soul has no death, if soul dies; nature loses its value hence nature keeps on producing billions of souls. Because nature by itself cannot understand Her beauty but souls can do so. Soul alone cannot understand this Nature but soul with its consciousness can understand this Nature better. That is why even if thousand nuclear bombs explode on the earth the very remnant of the soul remains. It is ever producing and everlasting. Because of this, the soul is a wonderful product and a creator's marvel. We cannot synthesise artificially the soul and even if we synthesise, it is detrimental to the very root of natural soul and the artificial cannot match the natural. When we start artificially synthesising the soul, world loses its existence. The transfer of this gene from one life to another life is otherwise called transfer of Nano souls, which is never ending, if soul ends then the whole universe ends. Here in the end too once again a new life starts through the remnant of soul what we have left. Hence soul is not there to look or feel and it has no end (infinite). Soul cannot be measured. When God has no death, soul too has no death.

If we believe in genetics or *Karma* of Hindu philosophy where all or some character, knowledge and behaviour pass through the genes from one generation to another generation so also in similar fashion one should believe in reincarnation too. How? Yes, I have my own view for the reader. It is like a computer where data is stored in folders and a click on the folder would get all the detail from that particular data. How can a person remember the past? Yes, a folder which hitherto is in a dormant state during the transmigration of genes in the past for thousands of years back, by chance is clicked by something (cue) on that particular folder would now release all the visual data as pictures of his past memory. A person in India, how can he remember his house at Russia? This is possible because if we think that we all are descendants from Adam and Eve that is we all are from one (today's billions of soul originated from one), our genes and their genes would have been culminated in the past during that great transmigration. It is akin to great transmigration of animals and birds. Therefore, *Punarjanma* or reincarnation should be viewed under a science perspective, not necessarily under modern *Swamijis* perspective. Further scientific research and pure understanding of this phenomenon of reincarnation would result in hypnotism as well as bogus propaganda of cheaters probably brings more clarification later when this false propaganda is viewed in a science perspective.

DASA

I have a friend; his name is *Das* and he is a very good friend of mine. When I was reading some literary books, I was really thrilled to know what *Das* means. If we know little *Purana* or *Vedantha* this *Das* means *Dasa. Dasa* is defined as mere submission to creator or God. *Dasa* in *Dasa Sahithya is a person who submits his Bhavana to God.* As per *Bhakthi* movement Purnandara *Dasa* a saint is one who completely submitted himself to Lord *Vittala, hence he* was a real *Bhaktha.* In the same fashion, Lord *Hanuman* was for his Master Lord *Rama (Karthavya Niste)*. In *Sankya* philosophy, this movement has been mentioned as friendship. Whatever may be the stories of this *Dasa,* he is one who seeks refuge with creator partially or totally. This is the best method to feel and see the God without spending much energy. No work ups, no books, no knowledge, no school or college and still we can go to the abode of creator. Effort needs energy. People do not waste their energy unnecessarily to know the creator. In this affirmative path to find and know the creator we require lot of energy and it is more time consuming. Spending energy to search the God is risky and stressful. Hence, people fall blindly in search of this creator. They fall to a dark canyon, bruise severely or die at times. This sort of tragedy we have seen and heard through news. Kindly understand what I explain, this is my explanation.

My friend Das would argue and as well blame his parents that he is a product of their sexual instinctive desire.

Poor Das does not understand why we worship god Kama and goddess Rathi. Sex is a symbol of love. Lust is a demon. As I have explained earlier, nature wants us for its existence. If by chance this parental sexual instinct dies, so also does this world. Nature wants always new souls to admire the universe and in the mean while Nature expects us to do something for this world which we never do. Creator has created wonderful humans and gifted humans with mysterious chemicals which work as chemistry or *Vasana.* As per the evolutionary reproductive theory, these chemicals work at the lowest level. That is how couples get blinded in love and in turn they mate. This mating cannot be stopped because of rich innervations of nerves in female genitalia and the culprit dopamine in male. In that orgasmic state, they forget the whole world because this state is hypnotic and in this euphoria they experience a total void. If *Das's* parents had foreseen about their son before their act of mating, Das would not have been on the earth because the very idea of him would make the father to suffer from erectile dysfunction and mother would have gone to a frigid state. This is the reason how we are all born to our parents. Why should we blame our parents? Mr Das never ends there; he would argue 'We are all born out of chance.' He is careful by not telling it by mistake. This mistake leads to controversy on legitimacy. Ignorant Das does not know the difference between duties and responsibility. Duty is dirty; responsibility is welcomed. His parents are responsible for his birth and his duty is to love the world so also responsible to look after his parents. This saga continues for ever as long as this world remains even after we shed our shirt and the soul escape in to this universe. It is Das's responsibility to know why he is born or what is the secret of him being born? If he knows, then he is a knowledgeable man and would not ask such questions. Having children is a real burden to parents; when we ask any parent, they would say, why did we had children! Today, because of burden, nobody wants to own a child, and that is why, single individuals are increasing in numbers. Long social stay and staying and forgetting attitudes are at an increasing trend, which has led to unseen and unheard psycho-social problems. Remaining as single would diminish the problems of responsibility. One should not shun the difficulties but find the enjoyment in those difficulties for their upward development; otherwise, they remain as childish, but not child-like. In urban society, divorces are at its peak because of many reasons. According to me, being thoughtless females and spineless males might be one of the many reasons.

MOTHER'S DAY

In the west, we have Mother's day and this has become the craze today in the east. People forget that in the east every day is mother's day. Nature also is called as mother because She gifted us. We are all born to mother, but the difficulty our mothers experienced is nothing when compared to Mother Nature who fought within her family comprising *Pancha Bhuthas.* They are water, fire, earth, air and sky (five elements). She has fought with her five children for thousands of years to get one amino acid or single life unit. This unit is an intelligent unit comprising not only the matter but also mind and it has survived against the destruction, reproduced again and again. If someone says his mother is everything, he has not understood motherhood and it shows his ignorance. Family values have come down because of this attitude where neo woman (bride) in that family is not considered as her daughter. This girl has been looked upon as a commodity. This attitude of commodity has been exploited by other family members. That is how families are fragmented. Basic reason for this is chemistry. A woman in that family does not share the chemistry of a new woman who comes later. This non-acceptance of chemistry leads to family anarchy and attendant family problems. Daughter is daughter for the woman at home but daughter of somebody is only daughter-in-law but not daughter in the real sense. This is what chemistry means to me. This is not one side story, vice versa is also true.

If this basic problem is not corrected at the earliest, the gap keeps getting wider and wider. Quarrels, fights, injuries, suicides, murders and divorces increase in many families due to basic disagreement on the said chemistry. This is not the only reason there might be many reasons but I think this chemistry is the main or major reason. This chemistry has been described in different terminologies in different books like signals, wrong message, ego clash, you-are-wrong and I-am-right, wrong processing and bio-socio and economic problems underlying psychiatric illnesses. This is an interesting field to be isolated and researched. My thinking is that there could be a gene, which could be found and isolated, by which a permanent cure on this basic chemistry could be possible. There also might be a centre in the brain, which can be stimulated so that a possible cure to basic disagreement could be a possibility as in the cases of intractable OCD's where cure could be expected by newly invented deep cerebral electrode stimulation of certain brain centres.

VIGHNA AND NIRVIGHNA

"Doctor you said *'Nirvighna'* the other day near a temple, please explain."

Did you see the board properly? It was *Nirvighna Vinayaka* temple. I had a young girl once in my clinic. Her *Bhakthi* towards her examination was great; still she failed, because her *Bhakthi* to *Raghavendra Swamy* was only to pass her exams without studying. When she had obsessed with her God; how could she concentrate on her studies? how could she score and pass her exams?

We are all royal beggars but not loyal beggars. A loyal beggar is one who begs loyally to meet his needs. A royal beggar is one who has everything but still begs. A royal beggar never misses to go temple, begging God for wealth, happiness and health. This royal beggar hides all these three and still begs. So, tell me, who is the thief? There is no difference between a real thief and a royal thief. This is a learned or conditioned art by religious wealthy people. The trend has changed now, people go to temple to beg and this begging has two types. One type is for their physical look, begging to look like Khans or six packs and to have eyes like Rai. Another type is for the mind. Have you seen any person in the temple to beg for his mind? Hardly, we come across such people. I am yet to see a person who begs God to make him a good person. He begs for his intelligence and this intelligence he uses to cheat people, uses to explode and destroy, uses to kill and cause agony. He asks the Lord to impart cunningness, to impart certain dangerous games, to impart some puzzles and from all these he can earn, he can extract money from others, he can deceive many and he can trick the fellow people. This is true with me also. Let us be frank in accepting. If there are no qualities of making money to a little extent, I would not have made wealth. Money is there with me only to look after me and my family with little extra luxury. I am not *Sathya Harishchandra* (King of truth) but what I want is that you can make the money but give correct service for money you take. This little money earned should bring contentment and share a part of this wealth with others if possible. This is what we have read, heard and saw with great Modern *Swamie's* who built huge empires and at last constructed schools and hospitals which are peanuts for the wealth they possess. People blindly fell to their trap, and in this milieu, followers have burnt their fingers by not recovering their thrashed money which would not be accounted after the death of such *Swamijis*. People tin in or share God with the money they acquire by illegal way. This is what exactly happens with Lord Thirumala. I have a friend who never misses *Thirumala* on *Vaikunta Ekadasi* and tin in or offers his 1% earnings. He is a poor doctor who helps needy patients charging moderate fees. Another friend is a son of a rich criminal lawyer and he is also of the same profession but offers 25% of his earnings because this criminal lawyer is sure that he would earn hundred times of what he has offered to Lord Thimmappa in no time. Both are happy; doctor has no money but rich mind and the criminal lawyer has money but no service. Hence, happiness is a common factor in both, but for the Lord the story is different. The Lord would appreciate both, how? If the doctor is recognised by the fellow people for his service and gets appreciated by his doctor friends. The Lord also appreciates the criminal lawyer if this lawyer shares his richness with the needy.

'Nirvighna' the very name in Sanskrit says "Go ahead, go ahead, I am with you, I will take care to see that you will come up in your life without any hindrances, go ahead with your adventure, I am behind you." Exactly, this is what happens in every ritual before we start our business. We invoke first lord *Vigneswhara* to provide or offer his *Nirvighna* in our business or our new venture. If I am having a big hospital, I would invoke first Lord Vinayaka. If I am starting a big hotel, then again I invoke first Lord Vinayaka; the bar owner also does not forget Lord Vinayaka. You can see Vinayaka's photo hanging on the wall of his bar. Brothel keeper also does the same thing. A thief or a burglar and also a murderer invoke Lord Vinayaka first in their venture. All have one common approach that is before they act on any kind of venture they would go to *Nirvighna Vinayaka* temple. They have beautiful prayers, they have double *Bhakthi,* and they all worship in a big way. Hence, what is the difference between me and these people? Lord is compassionate, throws his mercy to anyone who prays for Him; the lord does not differentiate the people, is also impressed by their prayers but look the propensity, the consequence, the outcome and the disastrous aftereffects. Is this what Lord Vinayaka ask for? We all know that here the object of worship is just a stone. Hence, this stone cannot punish the people who deserve punishment.

Why someone should punish us? Not required, why? Just listen to this story.

Worship is a ritual, prayer is *Manthra.* Worship and prayers are well taken up by the lord. Lord appreciates or pleased by *Manthra;* hence, people worship Him and offer their prayers to Him. It is beautiful to watch the rituals and to listen to their prayers. Compulsions and obsessions have rich ritual base. For an onlooker, this ritual is a treat to watch. Why people do this? "Fear, my friend fear," if there are any mistakes in the sequence of offering, anxiety creeps in. This anxiety is painful. It is a punishment. A thief has to sketch before he plans otherwise any mistake will have him caught. If a thief works with anxiety, he will be caught and subjected to punishment. The Lord never gave this anxiety, and this has come on its own. We borrowed anxiety from nowhere and if you ask OCD (obsessive compulsive disorder) people they explain what really anxiety means and how much painful the anxiety is. Anxiety is self-made and it is not made by others. Anxiety creeps in when a person is greedy, when he does wrong doings, when he wants to cheat or plans for a robbery or murder. The same phenomenon exists with a religious ritualistic man where he is always obsessed to visit temples. See a non-religious non-ritualistic man; he has no fear and also no pain. He is happy and tension free, hence nothing to fear from.

Manthra is melodious and impressive. Today, *Manthra* without melody has no meaning. From this melodious reciting technique by a conman, he tricks an ordinary man. An intelligent cheat has beautiful singing technique where he tricks everyone, make them go to sleep, and at this juncture, he collects all belongings intelligently from all those who slept. A hypnotist hypnotises onlookers and turns them in to a total *Nirvana* (wealth less) state except *Kopina* (cloth to cover private parts). I cannot chant, my chant is not melodious; hence, I am not a thief because I cannot induce others in to a state of sleep. Therefore, I cannot steal, rob or mug. My chanting is not melodious but my mind is melodious, so also my socio economic status which has remained poor. Lord Buddha remained as poor but his mind was very rich and illuminatingly rich. He was having nothing and he only had a little piece of cloth and a banyan tree as his home. He was in a state of *Nirvana*. He was untouched both ways. No one could touch or steal his mind. My mind is melodious; hence, people do not come to me because I am not rich. I am doubly happy as I do not have any thing for others to touch or steal. If I have valuables for others to touch and steal then how can I be happy?

One should wake up to see this paradox. Before any one tricks me to *Nirvana*, I am already at *Nirvana*. People points at me, laugh at me, cajole me, and talk about me because a trickster has already tricked me to *Nirvana*. Now I laugh under my lips, I laugh silently, laugh with understanding, laugh with melody because I do not get trapped and the great *Maya* does not have any role to play on me. I am at liberty, I do not have any bondage, I am at a total void person and I have not left any key for the illusionist to open my mind for him to play his tricks. So, I am happy and would remain happy. Therefore, no Lord leaves any sign boards at any religious places; it is we who put those sign boards. When the Lord cannot put those sign boards, where is the question of *Vighna* or *Nirvighna?* Both are with me. My *Vighna* says not to do ill, because it is bad. My *Nirvighna* says to do service, because it is good. So, my friends, because of this reason I love *Adwaitha*.

COMPLICATED TAP

"You said Complicated Tap but not Common Tap, what do you mean?"

Before proceeding to explain this phenomenon, I wish to make you know about something which is very interesting. Today you go the east or the west, yoga is the *Manthra.* There yoga means three. Firstly let us consider *Yoga Asana,* second the *Pranayama* and third is the *Dhyana.* First *Yoga Asana,* please tell me in what way it is different from ordinary country games? One is country and another one is an ancient type of play but this ancient play has become a recent commercial play called Yoga. I love to play country games but being an urbanite there is no chance to play it. I shall name a few of them, *Marakothi, Gilli Dandu, Bugari* and *Zoot Ata.* These games are a treat to watch, these games are played at villages and it is amazing to see how native players involve with their games. Because of urban migration, these rural native games and their playing techniques are fast vanishing. Their involvement in such games at village levels is unimaginable. True involvement and unconscious playing techniques of them in such games stretch player's muscles, ligaments and fascia. There is no burden on them. If these games are played against burden or consciousness, player's muscles do not stretch. Exactly this is the reason why women in our village do not experience pain even though pain exists because the exercise women undergo is natural and involuntary. Now look at the women who are in cities, their work at home or away from home are voluntary, hence a burden. The work, which they undertake, is showy; they think work as a duty but not as a responsibility. They do it for some purpose and expectations. For example, political women who work once a year as *Shrama Dana* in front of the camera to seek only the votes and it is a vote bank politics. Political men appease minority voters only to be elected time and again, and after getting elected, they forget the electorate. It is unfortunate to see that the minority remains minority even after sixty-eight years of our independence. The pains these women suffer are pseudo and exaggerated in nature. More like a conversion reaction (attention seeking) type. We have modern kitchens where women stand and cook. No squatting! They are addicted to TV, and spend most of their time watching TV. They spend more time in shopping but not at work. Their exercise is voluntary because these women go in search of coach or Yoga *Guru*. The modern coach does everything except what he has to teach. Being taught by the coach is not to my tunes, coaching helps at corporate level, as I am not competing I believe my natural play. Like a house constructed by an architect for you without your participation, it is an architect's house rather than your house. I want to have my own identity like Roger's free flow tennis. Roger requires a coach only to tune his mind but not for his playing techniques; he has a natural uninhibited involuntary playing technique. If Roger tunes his mind on his own, no coach is required. Hence, in these circumstances, I ask a question whether this pseudo-Yoga or the knowledge works. Yoga works only when there is involuntary, uninhibited, responsible type of work but not when voluntary, inhibited and duty like work. Therefore the work what I said should be illuminating and knowledge oriented.

Guru is there only to ignite initially and then in that light we have to find our own path of glory, to be liberated a little bit from many bondages, and lastly, which is very important, and that is to be more human. True yoga and knowledge are not different and the yoga, which a coach teaches, is more of false yoga. When a coach teaches you how to play is always a burden. Training by a coach is always voluntary and the stretch you learn from them is partial and not total. People should think twice before they should pay money for their partial stretch when it is not a total stretch. Whatever I am explaining here should not be taken literally.

In *Kriya* yoga, Pathanjali in his dossier says, it is not *Guru* but *Swa Adyaya* (self-study), which is necessary to free ourselves a little bit. Nowadays, modern *Gurus* incorporate this dictum and never teach their students. They just collect their salaries and forget their students. If they show any interest on a particular student, we have to think of the teacher's mind in an otherwise manner. Schools at villages are sanctioned with grounds. Students play more than reading, but in cities, schools are sanctioned with no playing grounds by means of bribing or by influence, so students read more when compared to play. City students succumb to too many new types of neurological fibro fasciae syndromes. Village students play cricket for fun but city students play cricket and watch cricket on TV for betting and match fixing. Presently, numerous Yoga Schools cropped from nowhere. Yoga *Asanas* have been taught indoors. Indoor asana is suffocating. Modern yoga teacher has no knowledge of asana but teach people because he is paid. If we question such teachers, they give several glorifying rosy pictures of cure for many physical and psychological ailments. The stories or explanations behind these *Asanas* are like chats and pizzas, which tastes well but in actuality they are junk and harmful to our health. I have asked questions to few coaches who teach yoga but I got schizophrenic answers in return. What answers you can get from an astrologer or a *Vamachari* (sorcery)? You get only foolish answers because only fools ask questions to them.

My sincere advice for any player is that, play a game with love but not with passion, play for yourself but not for gallery, play to your own tune but not to the tune of somebody else, play games from your heart but not for somebody else's heart and let your play come from within or involuntarily but let it not come from outside or voluntarily. Stress is a hindrance for your achievement; you may not recognise or shine immediately. It does not matter. Have patience and you will see later that it is not you who talk but your play talks. I love *Sapak Thakra,* watch the players, how they stretch and because when they stretch, stretch has its own beauty. I have not seen any game other than this game where players stretch their legs to perfection and this stretch according to me is beyond the limits of any game.

Pranayama is the second component of yoga. Brain has many functions and one among them is *Kriya* or *Karmic* or work. It is one among the four vital components of basic functions of brain. This is an elementary function of our life. *Pranayama* and *Kriya* go hand-in-hand in continuation of life. If *Kriya* or activity is more in you, your breathing also should be more. If you are a quiescent man breathing may not be required except to live. Increased breathing found in imperfect activity (example, under-prepared candidate facing an examination). In increased under prepared voluntary activity, breathing becomes difficult. Well prepared and professionals do not have the same difficulty in breathing and it is free flow. Breathing and oxygen saturation is innate with professionals. Their effort, lots of practice, their more patience and acquired knowledge works here. Without knowing what *Pranayama* is, *Pranayama* is just a breathing exercise. Hence, for the professionals and for people who have learned this P*ranayama* would accentuate their performance a little bit. For a non-performer and not learned person this *Pranayama* is a mere breathing exercise. Let me explain my view

Pranayama once again is voluntary under a coach. It is once again stress because you are breathing under watchful eyes. If you are watched, it is like putting a chain to a dog. You are not comfortable when you breathe to your consciousness. It is like heartbeat. Heartbeats are usually not perceived but palpitation is perceived which is painful. Hence, *Pranayama* is painful because it is done under watchful eyes. Look at the people who serve people in need, a doctor who has service motto and a literary man through his writing do a lot to society. A politician does good work for those who elect him. They all think it as their responsibility rather than duty. With responsible people breathing is involuntary and is smooth whereas people who think their work being duty, their respiration becomes jerky, not smooth, choking and are short in their breath. Carbon dioxide accumulates and lactic acid increases in their blood stream. He is clumsy, fearful, irritable and awkward. What is the reason? It is your ego; ego is the culprit and a master for all problems in human beings. With ego, you feel your work as duty and is voluntary but without ego, you think your work is responsibility and hence involuntary. Your ego keeps saying to you, "Why the hell should I work? What benefit do I have?" This negative thinking in your mind leads to uneven respiration, which makes you pale, you are disturbed, you are confused and your work gets halved. Basic principles of *Pranayama* have not been taught by the Yoga coach because the principal is different from other principles. Look at the paradox, a person who is having shortness of breath is already having high levels of carbon dioxide in his blood stream and now imagine he is doing *Pranayama* in an enclosed place where in this person keeps accumulating more and more carbon dioxide. I have seen masters of *Pranayama*, they choke when it really matters, choke in front of their wives and girlfriends. Remove your ego, you do not require a coach, you do not require *Pranayama*, because by removing the ego, you already have *Prana,* the knowledge and Yama the morality or ethos with all virtues and humility. Hence, your respiration is smooth and a free flow. My wife is a free flow type; she never does her household work as duty and always she thinks her household work as her responsibility. Because of this, she never goes to any *Pranayama* classes. There is no need for her. I have seen the art of living candidates. I have seen a woman who had attended art of living classes, kept her kitchen shabby not cleaned and smelling. I have seen another woman who goes to Yoga classes but she keeps poking her nose in others life. What is the use of going to such classes then? Today this ancient technique is limited to the breathing exercise in enclosed chambers. Please note and understand that these breathing techniques are required for those who work in high altitudes, for training athletes, for fire fighters, people who work in manholes and for the police force who fight along with shell bombs. It is unfortunate to see that all these people work under hierarchy because of which all these departmental employees lack quality. They work with fear, they are all chained dogs and they are kept under captivity. How can you expect the best out of these people?

No Olympic medal! This is because we are trained without breathing exercises; the police succumb to smoking and alcohol for the stress they encounter, fire fighter sleeps or plays cards because of inefficient equipment and the poor person who works in a manhole simply dies. Basic principle of *Pranayama* is to tune muscles and mind for low level of oxygen and to increase their working efficiency from the available oxygen what they inhale. Look at the disastrous management in our country. Does it exist? We have to search for these departments in our country. In simple words, you and I do not require *Pranayama* as long as our ego is under check. If this ego overtakes us, then *Pranayama* is required.

What is *Prana?* Many things have been explained by different people. Is it a sort of lymph or some kind of vital force? To tell you frankly, I do not know anything but I know something and that something is knowledge. I consider oxygen as omniscient and it is otherwise a living force in this universe. At present oxygen is the only vital element that has kept the life moving. You are dead without oxygen. Oxygen is omniscient; hence it should be a God; oxygen and God are the same. As per my understanding, this God is nothing but knowledge; so also is the oxygen. Therefore, I know two types of God spots or G-spots. One is situated at the top and another at bottom, which I have already discussed. G-spot down is primitive and studded with instincts. G-spot up is neo and more refined. This G-spot de facto or by default is not present at the top and this G-spot has to be acquired. This process of acquiring is affirmative, which requires persuasion and struggle. Hence, *Pranayama* is practiced through nose and nose upper vault is at the base of the skull, which is situated just under the forebrain or neo encephalon. Normally, all human beings respire by default, so automatically people take oxygen only to live. There is no conscious effort from the inhaler to inhale normal air, which contains oxygen. If there is conscious inhalation, then it becomes shortness of breath as in the mouth breathing. Hence, already you are taking God in some quantity to continue your life or soul. Let us say this soul is as a usual soul or normal soul. For a person who is born with normal soul, he does not want to live at that stage. Every living soul does strive to improve upon or transcend towards a liberated soul. In order to achieve illuminated soul, *Pathanjali* advised *Pranayama* as a part of one limb in his eight limbs. By each extra bit of breathing through *Pranayama* you are taking extra molecule of oxygen or otherwise extra God and thus extra knowledge. This extra oxygen or knowledge inhaled is stored in our neo encephalon or frontal lobe. Thus by long practice and understanding, we transcend G-spot lower down to G-spot up. If someone has the idea of Upanishad, *Udgaetha* or the breath has the highest value in the life. Meditating on that leads to *Jeeavana Mukthi* (free from life bondage). Speech, which is new, is considered as God and relatively old senses (five senses) are called as demons. Speech comes through breath. Hence, concentration, revitalising and thawing of this breath is called Pathanjali's *Pranayama.* This is the basic principle of *Pranayama.* Now breath has become a commodity as levels of carbon dioxide is increasing in the environment. You have to pay money to coach for extra oxygen under the name of *Pranayama.* People go to yoga classes only to beg for his or her physical health but not for mental health. This is what I regard unfortunate. You want more energy and a long life to have mean practices and bad thoughts to exploit and harm others. This is what I say 'bad to society.' Please enquire a coach what he means before he teaches any person *Pranayama,* I bet, he does not explain what breath is in a *Vedanthic* terminology and if you do not breathe, he is keep shouting behind you "Breathe deep, breathe deeper." Breathing without burden is nice and calm and the same with burden or under a coach once again is painful. Coach asks you to breath air in closed space, you think you are taking oxygen; no instead you are taking carbon dioxide. Go out and inhale air, you do not find oxygen, you have carbon monoxide due to motor pollution and in forest there are no trees hence only carbon dioxide, if you want to go mountains, they have been destroyed, hence no mountains. Do not listen to coach, do *Pranayama* wherever you are and inhale whatever oxygen is left, it is enough to survive but what you inhale oxygen is not refined one, once you refine and understand (allow Nature Mother to live), it is like understanding God or creator. Hence, understanding God is nothing but knowing knowledge. After this process, the knower becomes a person of knowing. Oxygen mixed with knowledge is accepting and only oxygen is nauseating, only knowledge is repulsive. Therefore, both oxygen and knowledge make a good cocktail, which tastes like a native nectar.

Coach under yoga has the last class, called meditation. What is meditation? Gurus and coaches give different versions or definitions of this meditation. In meditation, classes you see people who sit with their eyes closed. One definition of this meditation is that by closing the real eyes you open a hypothetical inner eye and start an inward journey to find what you are. However, I have seen people closing their outer eyes and opening their inner eyes only to find what material they have kept in their lockers. Inner eye searches for beautiful woman sitting in front or by the side of them. He opens his inner eye to sketch his next move to con or cheat others in business. Inner eyes open to plan for his next visit to meet his lover. Coach asks you to void thoughts. Ask a psychiatrist about this phenomenon; if somebody voids or has no stream of thoughts, he is fit to be called as schizophrenic. You cannot open your eyes, if you do so, your coach is at your back, and coach yells at you 'Close your eyes you fool.' It is a burden my dear friend, closing eyes is a burden. Meditate with your eyes open, it is not a burden and is more of a freedom. Meditation with burden is repulsive. *Mouna Muni* explains meditation as "Meditation is nothing but medication to one's own emotion" and also as "Meditation is compared to Mediterranean Sea. Look at the calmness it has, it is deep and blue, it has fauna and marine life, it has abundant knowledge within. Ask a young marine scuba diver, how much he is thrilled; he will not come out from the deep sea. He cannot acquire knowledge by closing eyes. If he closes his eyes, he would be killed by a passing shark, and such is the volume and value of this Mediterranean Sea, so also is the meditation." Now you understand the beauty of meditation. Meditator should open the eyes. He should be calm. He should be watchful. He should be a good observer and he should be available for a change or bend. If such qualities are there then he is practicing good meditation. Otherwise, meditation becomes *Jada Samadhi* or Pseudo-Meditation. Patience, practice and effort lead to meditation.

All these three would provide you the required calmness. In this calmness, your filters are shut to unwanted signals and are screened by the inbuilt servo mechanism of our body. Only the required signals go inside the mind. There is no short circuit in the brain and you will have time *(Samyama)* to process, to deduct logically and to reproduce knowledge from the memory storehouse whenever the world or wherever you call for.

Have you visited seven star hotels? Visit once. For a common man like me, seven star hotel is like a prison. I am scared to enter in side. Big lobbies, beautiful fountain, fantastic tiles, luxurious sofas, you might say "wow" but for me it is real scary. I have to talk and communicate in an alien language. I do not know where to go, which door to choose, whom to enquire and this causes real tremors and sweating. Both are masked by my loose pant and the hotels' central air conditioner. Hefty rent for the room, lavishly blended interiors, costly bed, bed sheet and towels, I feel like possessing them rather than spoiling them. Bathrooms are well designed with expensive taps. Find out or listen why I hate seven star hotels. Tap and commode are complicated and my urgency leads to confusion where my hurried nature call leads to bang my head and virtually I roll down. Hence, bathroom in seven star hotels is meant for very satisfied men but not for an ordinary man like me.

SURFER

It was a cool typical European beach where a friend introduces his techie friend to another friend who is an adventurous sports buff. "Tony, meet Pony a surfer." Tony looked at Pony "bingo, common man, sea is cool, wait till waves become big." Pony got astonished and went pale; Pony's friend could make out and read his expressions immediately, Pony, is an internet surfer. Tony realised that his friend's friend was a techie wearing bicycle pant not actually a sea surfer of whom he got confused with. Similarly, today we get prejudiced depending on our preoccupied mind in labelling some body. Why this story? As this world is going more technical, problems in managing illnesses are getting more complicated and this trend is increasing with IT and BT people. I have a drug *Carbamezapine* (anticonvulsant drug), which we use for certain types of epilepsies (fits). Today's techies are there everywhere irrespective of their places, villages or cities. They are great surfers and surf the internet. In days to come, we should hold internet surfing competitions between them. After surfing the internet for *Carbamezapine,* bystanders came to me with their arrows, guns and bazookas. I have to virtually shield myself or otherwise I would have perished just like Mohamed Gaddafi. Here, who is the looser? Both, I lose the patience, epileptic patient loses effective treatment. Look at the propensity of every day ordinary life. It is becoming more technical. Do we call this phenomenon being neo technological paranoia in modern interactive life? Belief has gone to dogs, today's world is still connected by belief but it is getting thinner and thinner and at one point of time world breakdown and thus we will meet an end *(Pralaya)*. I love sports, given the chance I would be a sea surfer than an internet surfer. Sport brings us solace and good healthy body. When we look at the present techies, stress and strain on them leading to unknown fibro fasciae syndromes to which orthopaedic surgeons have no answer. When we look at the amount of stress the technological people undergoing is a worrying matter. They are worried about their job cuts, layoff notices and what not. Similar way people do suffer in different ways, for example, Libya got liberated from dictatorship, but people of this country are facing problem of not having a good leader. On the other hand, in the developed countries people are trying to liberate from corporate inequality. That is why today people occupy Wall Street. Ultimately who succeeds and who perishes? We have to wait and watch. Throughout the world, this red force has the same theme but their attitude to bring this inequality is different as they tend to talk with their AK 47 guns. In today's world, whether this *Ahimsa Marg* or *Gandhian Principle* would really help this society at large is a big question.

WIFE MANTHRA

My friend said, "Look doctor, my wife is not happy about me," always she keeps saying that "No more I look attractive to you." In Kannada language, we have a proverb *"Doorada Betta Nunnige,"* which has a meaning that 'Neighbours grass looks greener than mine.' My friend is fed up in his life due to his wife's *Manthra* every day. For every moment, my friend spends his time with his wife is like hot ghee to him, he cannot swallow but, in the meantime, he cannot spit out. Why this kind of perception? I explained to him my view. There are three things for this phenomenon, which one has to remember. One is a 'domain'; another is a 'construct' and next is a 'theme.' First, one should understand the domain of forgetfulness. By and large, married woman forget that they have one domain called 'forget.' In my case, I love this domain because I am happy as long as I forget. If I start remembering then all my misery begins. I go on brooding. However, here it works exactly in the opposite way. Look here or observe carefully. She forgets how many times she has been smiled at by her husband and every time he smiles at her, she thinks that his smile is for the first time. This is an innate tendency of every other woman, which happens for the reason that she loves her husband true to her heart. This wonderful formula has been forgotten by her spouse. Any small, intended or non-intended smile to some other woman or man by either spouse leads to the repeat of the *Manthra.* Wife feels that husband is like a fellow who eats *Jamoon* every day, which tastes no good after eleventh day. She forgets that there is celibacy or resolution phase to coup up and deliver the same next time. Love is there but action and exhibition are not there. So when pleasing is an action then the act of lovemaking is also an action, hence, morality here is just to be accepted. This is what exactly the *Thanthra* explains. *Thanthra* is not the knowledge but it is the observation. Silent observation allows us to realise. Understanding and realisation leads us to accept. Therefore, both should accept and this acceptance leads to silence in the family. If not then we see turmoil at home. Hence first reason for this ruminative *Manthra* is 'Domain of forget.'

Next is a "construct of time." Woman in the family fails to analyse how much time she was with her husband and interacted. Now, she does not forget and also she has lost the analysing capacity of this time, when both problems persist, her *Manthra* keeps repeating because whenever she is with her husband she always feels that it is for that moment only.

Third is "theme of knowledge" which plays a major role. Knowledge of women is verily low; her discriminative power has taken the back seat. She forgets 'universal love' because she is already in a state of not forgetting, her remembrance is at its peak, and she has no time sense. She does not understand the give and take policy for which knowledge is prerequisite. Can anybody be a stone face for some body? This is exactly what I want to say, give and take principle. If we smile to someone, automatically we are smiled at. That is what her spouse does but it is being mistaken for the want of knowledge by her. Whatever said and done, the smile or greeting should not possess any lusty qualities. If that lust is the principle source of interaction, wife has every right to question her spouse. When all these three qualities do not work or work together the wife *Manthra* might remain permanently or temporarily.

ATTRACTION

We all get attracted to the external world of living to non-living things, something to everything, stone to diamond, hut to bungalow, and so on and so forth. This attachment in a social animal like us is a necessary quality to move forward. Attraction is good for a person as long as it remains as an attraction but when the same attraction gets conditioned it gets converted in to obsession, and then this obsessive attraction leads to many miseries in our life. For some, this obsession becomes a compulsion, and at certain time, these compulsions can get converted in to impulsive behaviours, which in turn lead to psychiatric disorders. This tendency allows a few mind sets into biases or prejudices. This bias remains in such minds, until something called recognition comes in the middle. After recognising the prejudices, this prejudice has to be pulled up, cleaned and shown to the light of discrimination. This process of cognition is otherwise called reasoning. These biases and prejudices have to be debated in the court of consciousness for our clear conclusions.

Attraction and repulsion are the two attributes, which are like two sides of a coin, and they are the basic necessity for the Law of Life to exist. At the same time, they are the good breeders of misery, which leads to unhappiness in our life. Why misery? Because both have very strong binding forces, charged with energy. Both are equipotent, but in my view, repulsion is more dangerous and very strong when compared to attraction. A person can overcome attraction not necessarily repulsion. Attraction can be transcended, but not repulsion. In the path of *Vairagya* (renunciation), one should first concentrate on repulsion *(Dwesha)* to thin out for a blissful life later. Hence, freedom from both is a hallmark to be a true Yogi. This learned state by a seeker is like a state like relishing a *Jamoon.*

REPRESSION

Enlightened master once said, "My dear friend, do not harbour repression, repression is the root cause for many problems." Yes, in one way, this master is correct and in another way, the same master is wrong. Let me explain. This is my view. We have two laws, one governed by the present law, which keeps on changing and to put it right as Statutory Law. This law is not permanent in the present context. Another law is Natural Law, which is eternal or permanent and is governed by universe or *Brahman* and the same is otherwise called as Universal Law. Now what governs most, whether Statutory law or Universal Law? Statutory law holds good for our wrong doings under a framework of particular society of that country but Universal Law holds for social wrong doings. We are taught only Statutory Law but not Universal Law. Hence, we concentrate only on Statutory Law for our benefits but not universal law because it benefits the whole world. Therefore, once again it is 'I' rather than 'we.' We have constructed beautiful bungalows, living and eating lavishly. Do we find the same with all in this earth? There are many who are shelter less, cloth less and starving which shows that what an inequality exists in terms of social justice under Universal Law. This in turn has led to universal social unrest, which has led to loss of innocent lives; property worth millions and billions of rupees has been lost in the name of terrorism, there exist civil wars, naxalism is growing and social anarchy is at its increasing trend. Who gains? It is loss only to the taxpayer, loss to this world, loss to the kith and kin. Can we bring back the loss? No, if we understand the pulse of social injustice only then we can bring back those losses. We never try to understand the psycho-social explosion of inequality. Thus, Statutory Law cannot solve this huge problem. This can be solved only through deep understanding. We should get equipped with good instruments and scales to overcome such huge differences with good compassionate adhesives to fill the crack, which we have already created. By using refined and defined equipment's many problems could be solved. Whole world can be happy if we adopt such qualities. Such mechanism is not with us individually and in the same time, that mechanism is present with every citizen to vote for a good leader to bring good government and governance whose *Manthra* is to meet the social inequality.

Let us try to understand another type of repression, which has led to many problems in our society. There is a group of people who are against Natural law but not Statutory Law. They are basically human beings but they differ from others by their nature of function. Until now, they were living behind the walls. They got segregated by fearing social values of that country or place. They are repressed as well as fearful for no fault of theirs. They are out casted people in our tradition. Their behaviour is taboos' in our society. They are not allowed to move in our culture and they themselves do not mix with us. They have their own identity; hence, they are forbidden in our culture. They were used by some people as agents for their urges and few notorious mafia groups as marketing commodity to earn money. Their life starts in the dark and ends up in the morning. They remain underground the whole day.

After several debates with the government, human rights activists, NGO's, judiciary and liberals, government wants to bring all these people under a common forum. After bringing them at par with the public, how the change was viewed? Some view this as a political conspiracy and others view it on humanitarian grounds. Whatever may be the reasons, one should understand the problems, which arise between normal to abnormal. Are they fit to be called normal? However, as per Natural law, they are not normal, as per statutory law they are normal. How? Now look at the *Brahman* or *Prakruthi* (world), which always wants micro *Brahman* (soul) or *Purush* (man) to address or to admire *Ago Brhaman* (universe). If all of us become hermaphrodites, gay or lesbians then what is the purpose of this very existence of nature. Nature wants life to continue, when this life does not continue then there is an end to this existence. In such conditions, nature starves and its work ceases. Does nature want this? Definitely, nature does not allow this to happen. Nature wants life to continue. Hence as per the Law of Nature, this repression is correct, but it is vice versa under the statutory law. Law is amended, Government showered voting rights on them, they can mix with others, nobody should insult them, and they can work with us. At the same time, there is every possibility that their illegal activities might increase during daytime; hitherto it was during night times. NGO's are happy but at what cost? The pain people experience, when they are near to them (in many traffic junctions and in railway stations). Frankly, I am not against them on any count and I am as concerned as any enlightened human but where is the threshold to accept or not to accept? These things have to be addressed by each and every one. As their number keeps on increasing, politicians are the beneficiaries as they get their votes. If we want to be *Shivayogis* we all should be born here in nature to experience lord Shiva. Now, from the Statutory Law, the repressed are made to experience lord Shiva, actually this lord Shiva is not happy. Politicians are happy, NGO's are happy but I am happy and also unhappy.

KRISHNA

A young psychiatrist had just finished his MD in Psychiatry from a prestigious institute and had started his private practice. He was enthralled by reading *Bhagavath Geetha.* He wanted to include ancient epic story themes in his counselling sessions. His first counselling session to counsel was regarding conduct disorder. Psychiatrist asks his client "Who is Krishna my dear?" Client said "One who does difficult *(Klista)* problems at ease with ones cunning intelligence *(Chanakshathana)* is called *Krishna.*" Doctor went dizzy by his clients answer. Actually, he was counselling the patient Master Krishna who used his intelligence with mighty cunningness and certain mind games to take advantages from his parents and also from cheating friends. He was utter nuisance in the family so also in the public and if by chance he had used his intelligence for constructive works, he would have been a pearl in his family. There was no need for the doctor to counsel him. Doctor perspired over his answer, with hurry and burry by giving some vague reason he ends the counselling session by telling 'Keep it up.' This client, Master Krishna, kept this bachelor degree of cunningness only to become a rich and famous minister to amass and store illegally taxpayer's money and also became richer through grabbing the wealth of his state. After several years of collecting such wealth, he as a minister later became the chief minister. The psychiatrist wanted to take advantage of this opportunity. He wanted to give a representation to this chief minister for sanctioning a small piece of land to construct a small hospital. Doctor being simple and dedicated went to meet this chief minister in his casual dress with an ordinary look. Doctor was hoping that this chief minister would recognise him as he had counselled him earlier. Minister recognised doctor physically but not intellectually. He was made to wait until evening. Doctor's repeated enquiries went to deaf ears and in turn got dumb answers. Minister asked his marshals to handle this doctor diplomatically. Doctor got frustrated and left the premises. Later, he never discussed with any one regarding his visit. After all, the doctor wanted a due recognition, which he did not get. Minister knew the purpose of doctor's visit through his post-graduate degree of cunningness. Poor fellow returned to hometown with the same old beard and Hawaii's. Moral of the story is that people's representatives always swear oaths to be like Lord *Krishna.*

BRAIN HOME

"Why do you call brain, a home? Please explain doctor."

This question is occasionally asked to a neuro-psychiatrist. Yes a home, a big home and also a complex home. This home is non-understandable one. In the urban world, you have many such houses. No one comes out or enters this house and it is always closed without knowing the occupants identity and also their whereabouts. These types of homes are ill understood. I have a colleague who never invited me to his house warming ceremony. His mind is a complex in nature, which you and I cannot understand. As my colleague cannot come out from this complexity, I cannot enter his complex home. Exact opposite to this nature, I have another colleague who took me to his house. It is a big house and really complex in nature. Many rooms, halls, living rooms, movie hall, etc. and it cost him crores. He took me to his kitchen and it was a big kitchen with very expensive fittings and materials. I failed to understand his complex because he never allowed me to touch any material. Only two of them stay in that big house and by profession both are doctors, they never cook food in their kitchen because they are always busy attending their patients, hence both always eat food outside. So in each one of us in this universe have different kinds of complexes. One is simple and another one complicated. Friend's kitchen became a showpiece, a mere showpiece.

In a similar fashion, my brain is a big house with many kitchens, many rooms, many living rooms, etc. However, all these kitchens and rooms function unlike my friend's kitchen which is always a show piece. This big house, which houses so many rooms and kitchens, to what extent they work under any given point of time is important. Some are quiescent but still function and some are more active. This depends on each individual. This mystique brain-house houses parents and many children including servants. Each has a separate room and in actuality some rooms do not open at all, closed from inside with their children alone who have internet access. Imagine what could happen to these children.

Exactly this brain has millions and trillions of rooms, some locked and some open for the parents, brothers and sisters. Brain houses four important people and they are thoughts, feelings, will and actions. Each one of them greets compliments and works together just like in any other house. If our house does not function with togetherness, imagine the chaos the house would undergo. The same holds good with the brain home too. They all work together; if they work differently, there will be total anarchy and huge confusion and madness in the process. Hence, they are interrelated and interconnected. Father has to greet mother, in turn to children before they leave for work. If father does not, he will have the prize when he returns home from his work. Here also thought should communicate and say hello to each one of them before he comes out because all are related. If one gets angry, there is a disconnection between them, hence a split exists. This split is called schizophrenia. So there should not be prejudices and no taking sides. There should be equal distribution of love and feeling. If not, action gets angry; person becomes irritable, destructive, agitated and violent. The feeling goes for a depression. He becomes dull, apathetic and does not work. The 'Will' have no vision, fail to find a good path as he is more confused because 'Feeling' is not with him. He becomes drive less. Thought, which always expresses in the form of words, has few words or no words. Even if he has, it is broken and there 'Formal thought disorder' exists. When 'Thought' wants to have a breakfast, he has to call 'Feeling' too, if he has not called 'Feeling,' 'Feeling' would sketch a plot to teach the 'Thought.' At times, even if 'Thought' wants to be apologetic to 'Feeling,' when he tries to call him 'Feeling' would have closed the door and any amount of begging would not help in bringing him out. Hence, one should be very cautious in exchanging compliments. In this milieu of taking, giving, complimenting and sharing, there will be regulation of chemicals, which keeps man upright. If these chemicals lose regulation, then real madness comes in. Psychiatrist is ready to receive them for treatment, and at times, it is beyond psychiatrist's management to bring him back to normalcy. Regulation depends on give and take principle. A big house like brain should have harmony of humours to keep mind and body in tranquillity. Kitchen should function and it should not be ornamental. Otherwise, smile becomes ornamental, as an artificial smile. If the smile possesses warmth, that smile is from the heart. When all these functions work united and in a congruent or coordinated manner, you have a home sweet home.

OBSESSION YOU STARVE

I have explained earlier that our habits do not die easily. Habits can be dangerous when they turn into obsession. Would we like to live with an obsessive? I know, all of us tell no. It is difficult to have relationship with perfects. Behavioural therapists make a lot of money because hard core obsession is like an ostrich egg. Professional psychologists and psychiatrists find it very difficult to crack this ostrich egg. Irony is that the person, who harboured already an obsession, develops another obsession of distrust. In this way, the patient does not trust the doctor and the doctor does not trust the patient because the patient may not pay fees to the doctor for his non-improvement. We live in these types of obsessive plays, some are simple and many are more complicated. Hence, life is full of neat dramas. Obsession of clean, germs in the plate, dirt with chef and server contains dangerous organisms in their cooking and serving hands, etc. leads to suffering due to starvation. No glucose to brain, head gets dizzy, clouded, weak and irritable. Therefore, obsession leads to starving. Thus, I leave it to you; if obsession is not a disease, choose obsession or food.

GAMES WE PLAY

"Please high light the games we play, doctor."

Yes, it is all in the games we play. Games we play between hierarchies between the rich and the poor, between our relationships, between scientists and spiritualists, between secular and pseudo-secularism, between politics, and so on and so forth. We play games for our survival. Survival to lead our life, survival to be live big, survival to get attached, survival to make more money, survival to acquire knowledge, etc. These games are more complex when compared to the usual games played in a playground. Games we play in a playground are refreshing and stress relievers but these games played outside the playground are dangerous and stress enhancers. The games we play on the ground are straight forward, not cunning and always transparent and straight. These dangerous games we play outside are non-transparent because we are masked or covered. People are more cunning because games played are not direct or face-to-face. They are behind the doors and there exists a veil between players. These dangerous games are played on top, down or from behind but not from front. These games are camouflaged and they could ambush us easily. When the attack is from the back, no one can escape. If attack is from the front one can escape. Living, earning and cheating are all games that we play, so also flip pops and lullabies. Cunning to subdue, greed to amass wealth, down play to be prominent, colourful to be a celebrity, yielding to have favours, etc. are all in name of different games. Mind games are complex in nature. I hate chess for this reason. Chess is one game where we sketch or premeditate to kill queen and king. In this game, before you move a pawn, you have thoughts of future traps and have calculations just to kill. All games we play in the playground are instantaneous, reflex oriented, no calculations and no premeditation by any player. Watch football, where there are high emotions, quarrels and fights are instantaneous and they forget then and there. But, in the games we play, they will have lot of premeditations and we are destined to trap and kill. In our statutory law premeditation carries the highest punishment but in the game of chess you have the highest reward. I hate this game. This is my view and others need not carry with the same attitude. All other games are influenced with weather, pitch, ball, shoes, clothes, place, indoor or outdoor and other equipments but the game of chess does not have any such preconditions except player's mind which has a complex game structure. Hence, if your mind is sketch oriented, trap oriented and camouflage oriented, you will win. For all such games of harming someone, modus operandi is our brain. If a player does not possess these attributes he loses. I do not have these qualities hence I hate this game because I cannot win. This is the only game that has wood, porcelain, marble, silver, gold boards with king of diamond, queen of platinum. I do not have silver, gold and platinum; hence I do not play chess. Friends, do not think that I hate this game but in life this type of chess game, I hate. This is the only game that pulls or blocks other players' mind. He has ample time before he makes a move. That is why it is sketch and trap oriented. Let the people in society play understanding games and let this cunning, trap, calculative games stop and start to improve others mind to fight, talk and work against the evil. Let the games to be God-like, full of fragrance, more subtle. Let the game be true in all its expressions and also in its spirit, the spirit of love, spirit of non-hate, spirit of not troubling. So kindly join my new party "not to trouble others" party.

"More about these games please."

Very interesting, I know all of you are interested. Look at your family; I know you never look at your family because we always look at neighbour's family or distant relative's family or friend's family who are rich and famous. This is our innate engineering marvel which has to be shed. I am not blaming any one because this tendency has travelled along our genes from generations to generations from our forefathers. Now I give you a day just to watch and to look at your family. If you do so, you would come to know the different varieties of games. They range from small to big, easy to complicated, mild to severe and calm to dangerous. Only thing you have to do is just sit and watch, be still, be calm and be meditative. Try one day; you will say I am right. Family has many members, father, mother, grandparents, brothers and sisters. Now your work is just to watch the games, which they play with each other. I told you earlier that we are not calm or still because we take sides, we are prejudiced, we keep moving from one court to another court depending upon how strong and how well family players play or plan these games. All these games we play are only to survive, to win, to lose, to yield, to take favours, to cheat, to con, to dominate, to maintain hierarchy, to snub, , to make one a slave, and so on and so forth. These games we play only to be egoistic, to be submissive, to dominate, to lose or to win. Ultimately, no one gains, no one loses, and I have seen the big and muscular lose and the puny winning. We keep hovering between villains to heroes. Go to the history, you can read what happened to the Martin King Luther and Gandhi? What happened in the war between America and Vietnam? Only weak could win and it is all in the game. The weak played his game of good and nonviolence; it is a sort of disguise. Camouflage through well planned ambush worked in Vietnam against the strong; this is once again an intelligent game from which the weak can win over the strong. *Ahimsa Marg* is a type of game played and it worked for the weak by compassion. See, these types of games and all are totally different and exactly opposite with different dimensions. It is said games should not be esoteric, but should be exotic or exciting, truth oriented; naked and if that is so then one can see games with harmony and not with psychophony. The player who plays game realises good only when he is in perfect totality on stillness. This understanding by a good player comes from total emptiness and that is how Buddha attained *Nirvana.* Modern yogis do play games but fail miserably; they do not know what is in a game? They do not play true games but they play dangerous games. They cannot even talk of true games because games they play are cunning and conning. There is no difference between a child-like game and Buddha game because the game children play has innocence; child gets angry but that angry has a meaning. Adults too get angry but they have a meaning of different connotations. These meanings could be greed, lust, favour, etc. Buddha never got anger but lived with that anger, while living he realised and understood the anger. That is how he was conditioned to do only good. Transformation or transcendence was filled in his mind.

There was no scope or space for anything except love, peace and tranquillity. That is the beauty of Buddha.

Look at the interactive games of mother playing with the father, where the father is playing with the mother only to win, to win the love, and to win dominance. You should be watching it. To watch one requires silence and emptiness. If not, you lose everything. If you are not observing you get defeated. This is what happens with our children who play game with their parents overtly or covertly. They are vehement at times; subdued other time, apply rules and regulations another time which lead to disastrous end. I will tell you a story if you are empty, friend; Listen to this story of two sons. Father is pious, well taught, a professor, good orator, highly philosophical from an orthodox family who mastered Vivekananda teachings, married late and had two children. The elder is brilliant; always questions his father and others but father never questioned his son for his eating habits, which led him to put on lot of weight. He did a professional course, shuns people probably a complex personality and always stayed at room reading all philosophical books available on earth. He attached to his uncle who was not married and he was a type born to nurse his mother who was ill at that time. Uncle was like modern Nachiketha who pleaded Lord Yama the king of Death to give back the life of his mother to him. The elder son of this professor was confused, after addressing his father and his uncle he left with confusion to choose, with whom or to which type of player he has to join whether uncle or father. Years passed and he felt that it is better to be like a Buddha. Therefore, he never mixed with any one and went to silence without being illuminated. This led to disastrous ending of confining permanently to his bedroom after the death of his younger brother. His younger brother is exactly the opposite of him. He is outgoing, fantastic net surfer, spent all his time only surfing the net whole night, never came out in the morning, never attended the college, brilliant in his speech, good at English, was putting across the philosophy to the point perfect and was crystal clear in his explanations and also in his arguments. But his main arguments were towards *Shoonya* (zero). He was not at all tangible but spoke only to an end point. He believed firmly that he would come back in another *Avathar* after his death. This son of this professor was *Vedanthic* and a prolific half philosopher without sufficient maturity. He asks his father to get him a guitar. He was not satisfied with an ordinary guitar, he wanted an electric guitar, but without the knowledge of what that guitar is, he would half master it immediately but never pursue it. He wants a camera and the same old story repeats. An expensive camera becomes worthless in a few days. Father never questions his son, because he knows his son is very intelligent and if by chance father asks a question to this son, he would reply father with filthy language. Hence, parents stopped questioning him. Parents are mute spectators to his deeds. Parents did not take anybody's advice; if they take then they had it. Eldest son pours water to the floor and asks mother to clean the floor as punishment. The second son would argue with his father whole night with all the words in the dictionary for which father had no answer. This father was scared and also happy about his second son. Father is happy because the knowledge this son possess was more but scared to question him because he would lose his son. With that confusion, he spent days and one day he is a spectator for his younger son who met a horrific end or point of no return of a ghastly accident where his bike collided with a road side tree at a speed of 120 k/hr under the influence of two bottles of vodka inside his stomach. After that event his elder son got isolated and became paranoid and confined himself to his beautiful world of books and his mystique world. Elder son of this professor found solace and happiness with the interactive virtual games he played through the internet. See the game they played in their family. Games of confusion in upbringing, blackmailing parents, demanding for costly things, incorrigibility, coercive, inadequate approach to children, philosophical without knowledge, scary living by parents, parents not taking advice from professionals, and so on and so forth which led to a disastrous ending. All the games they played were without understanding, no involvement and no acceptance but if these criteria were not there, no doubt they were worthy to the people or good contributors of wisdom to the society. This professor was like Buddha to his children, he was a blind witness to non-flow pyro techniques of his children. He never uttered a word, and in turn, he appreciated his children, first son ate like *Bakasura* (demon who eats nonstop), the professor is cool, the second son paints their living room wall like *De Vinci* or *van Gogh,* the professor is cool. The professor failed to hold the children either with a chain or rubber rope because if they flee to a point of no return, with the imaginary rope he could try to bring them back. It never happened because professor talk's freedom of their children and in this philosophy of chaotic games of freedom children played dirty games in his family; ultimately down fall was the answer. When professor was questioned about all this, he talked of *Vidhi* (fate), he gave lectures on that. See the game of this irony, which ended with tyranny. See these games, who wins? Who loses? And ultimately everything ends in zero.

The whole world is like a huge theatre in which all of us are actors. There are heroes, villains, heroines, conmen, cheats, jokers, etc. and also the characters of god-like. If a theatre is full of good actors then think of that community. The country would really prosper and become rich not by wealth but also by knowledge. Hence, play games that are suitable, play games which are useful, play games which are beneficial. Let the game help for those who are not transformed or transcended and the game we play should be like 'not to trouble others.'

MOTHER

I have a friend who lives next to my house. He is a good man and God-like and I am lucky to have him. He is a doctor by profession. Always smiling and interacting. He has a widowed mother who has sensory neuronal degeneration of eighth nerve bilaterally. She hears low frequency sounds but deaf for high frequency sounds. She is a very intelligent old woman who is able to grasp all low frequency noises but pretends as though she has not understood anything. She would have come to know everything beforehand, except a few. Her attention increases her hearing capacity. She harbours paranoid ideas with referential thinking due to her sensory impairment. If daughter-in-law shouts at her, mother-in-law thinks she scolded her, if daughter-in-law speaks with low frequency voice, this mother-in-law thinks her daughter-in-law is making some comment on her. But, the old woman's son is Buddha like. Months and years passed, still the neighbour is a Buddha. Always silent and enjoying those scenes. His advice to both did not help. He was definite that communication, signal processing and over tone are at fault. But, this neighbour was still smiling and laughing. They were adamant and incorrigible; still he was happy and not minding. No question of yielding by both, therefore always quarrelling. It was like taking an old man to a physician regarding excessive drinking and smoking. Physician would advise the son "Look my friend give him two pegs more and five cigarettes extra." The physician knows he cannot do anything for this old man. Habits die hard, I have a tennis mate who has TAO (thrombo-angitis obliterans) but he never stops smoking. Another friend of mine, who is in a habit of taking whisky, would shout *"Arre Whisky"* instead of *"Arre Isky"* when he misses the tennis ball while playing rallies.

I could not stop my neighbours smiling and laughing. It was amazing for me why my friend keeps on smiling and laughing even when there was a *Kurukshethra.* I wanted to know about this amazing behaviour of his. He is a good man and I am pretty sure that my friend is not a schizophrenic because for an observer who does not know this man mistakes him for schizophrenia because he laughs and smiles to himself which are the hallmarks of schizophrenia symptoms. One day it so happened, he was leaning to my compound wall and after a brief period of pleasantries between us, I asked him, "Why do you smile and laugh?" He was unperturbed, very calm in answering my question. "Dear doctor, you want to know why I smile and laugh," "Yes" I said.

"What is male hormone?"

"Testosterone,"

"What is female hormone?"

"Oestrogen,"

"What does oestrogen do to the heart?"

"It protects the heart and prevents heart attacks."

"That is why I laugh doctor. If I weep, I lose one day of my life, when females weep, nothing happens to them. Women fight but nothing happens to them. When women are angry nothing happens to them and everything happens with only men who possess testosterone. As I have no oestrogen, I want to keep my heart safe; hence, I smile and laugh." What an idea *Sir Ji.* The answer is a food for thought.

YOU ARE INNOCENT, YOU ARE FULL

Look at the above statement, it means nothing to you; you have to go a little deep. Fire as such does not hurt you but emotions after fire hurts you. Fire that causes burns on your body is not producing pain to you, but pain inducing Amines or release of Kinins is the root cause of your pain to say that it is pain. What happens to a profound mentally retarded? He is like Master Buddha, at total *Nirvana* who catches fire like a butterfly, so innocent where he never withdraws his hands, mother has to pull his hand out, and this Master Buddha notices pain only when Kinins starts working. He cries and never tells that it is because of fire. He is innocent my friend. Be full and be innocent that is what hypnotism does. Get hypnotised, you feel numb, where in this state the dentist is happy to perform any sort of manoeuvrable surgery. The patient is happy so also the dentist. Hence, be meditating on anything and be full, people never hurt anyone and what hurts them are feelings. Refine feeling, thaw it, break it, see what is red and green, throw away the red and keep the green. Move on and be free flow, in this, look for a change like Buddha. The Buddha got enlightened after many years of mental suffering while searching for good. Feeling pain is mind pain unlike body pain. Mind pain is really painful. You can sustain body pain but not mind onslaught. That is why few people die quickly. What a loss to people around the fellow who commits suicide? What a great loss to this country and waste of life? It is mere belief which takes you to trance, so also one's only belief can prevent this drastic step of losing life or ones agony my friend. Obsessions are for intelligent who are greedy, obsession comes first to any striving person like obsession of faring well, obsession of recognition, obsession of becoming rich, and so on and so forth. No end dear friend, these are the root causes of our misery. Innocence is the opposite of obsession, be watchful, be full and you have everything at your feet, no hurry, hurry ruins you, you will have bruises and fracture, avoid hospitals spending money. Nowadays orthopaedic surgeons are expensive. If you are obsessed, you starve because you are obsessed with dirt, not clean, not washed hence starving. How could anyone expect serving plates should be clean and neat to cent percent? Be innocent to have full stomach. Starving leads to weakness, no energy and only suffering. If your stomach is full, no such problems are noticed. The love, the compassion, the fragrance from the heart comes through mind full, which leads to healthy thinking.

Heart should be full like Lord Hanuman (monkey god). Master is Lord Rama but Hanuman is a great servant full of passion and love for his master. You have many temples of Lord Hanuman and these temples have outnumbered Lord Rama temples in our country. You have a dog in your home. Dog is your servant and you are the master. Dog's demise leads to a total grief in you. Your wife's death leads to grief but not real grief. Why? Because, your dead dog is full in your heart. That is why a dog has been worshiped as Narayana. It is the *Niste* (faithfulness) or the servant attitude, which has made people to worship dog.

With *Ahankari* (egoism) the heart is not void, no place for good as mind is already occupied with worldly attachments. In the *Nirahnakari* (egoless) heart is full of passion and no greed. Such *Nirahankaris* you find them in Golden Temple, they are 6 and ½ feet tall, weighs 100 to 120 kg, they greet you, they smile at you, they are at your feet to serve you. Why and how? It is all because the heart is full of service. If your heart is full, you are child-like and not childish. There is abundant difference between child-like and childish like. Think over what you want to be, obsession or no obsession, full or not full, I leave it to you.

When your heart is full, there is nothing to take and it is only to give, leave wealth and take compassion. Keep doing it and one day you attain *Nirvana,* a transcended or a little illuminated and keep doing it further more and more, you are a little liberated, there is nothing to give and take, go still further and in that state you are free from *Raga* and also from *Dwesha.* This ultimate state been exactly called as *Jeevanamukth,* do not hurry. You will not get this state tomorrow. This process takes place from generation to generation, generations of going up but not coming down. Refine, my dear friend. If you do so, you have better progenies; future generations of yours will be good. After all, you are leaving your thrashed money and material for your children but this money and material go waste if they do not elevate in their thinking. Therefore, start doing it now what I explained to you, do not waste time my friend.

A teacher just teaches, but a master not only teaches but also makes teaching understandable to his students. Therefore, teacher is knowledgeable but still not knowing, hence knowing and knowledge are different. If the master has only knowing, his *Ahankara* (ego) changes to *Nirahankara* (egoless). His mind is empty and in this emptiness and stillness he receives everything, his acceptance increases and he is highly perceivable. When this state is attained, then automatically his heart is full and pure. That is how *Nirahankari* becomes a child. When this child-like state is reached, the ritual begins. And that ritual is *Peta Dharana* (decorating with Mysore *Peta*) and *Shaalu Dharana* (covering shoulder with Kashmir shawl). See the beauty of these rituals, nowadays it has lost its value and also lost its ground, because these rituals are done for those who are *Na Layaks*. Still people are there in this world who are fit to get honoured but those who have to be rewarded are very few and are not recognised.

At Home In Front of Plate

AT 2 Pm,

Away From Home Finding The Plate,

Obsessed You Starve,

Innocent You Are Full.

Prima facie, this parable appears schizophrenic or as formal thought disorder for a reader. My professor at NIMHANS would address his students as, "You schizophrenic (professor never meant literally, my professor expressed this once after observing my hand writing)." Yes, all are schizophrenics, you know why? Understand carefully. We all have one full non-split brain. What is schizophrenia? Split mind is the answer (schiz is split and phrenia is mind). What is split? It is not physical split. Hence, split should be something else. It cannot be in its structure but only with its function. What are the functions of the brain? Mainly four, they are thinking, emotions, will and action. All these four functions should coordinate properly. They should work in congruence and if there is any asynchrony between these four in their execution, then schizophrenia exists. To give an example, see our *Netas* who promise one thing in their manifesto and execute nothing after winning. Are they not suffering from schizophrenia? Likewise all of us are schizophrenics one or other time. We are all mad who ranges from 1% to 100%. Near to hundred one lands up in psychiatric hospital and near to one has a happy life. Ask somebody "What is mind?" Answer would be a bundle of thoughts. This answer is from professor and if he is a scientist, the answer would have been bundle of thoughts are secondary to bunch of signals. These signals arise from environment, from moving world but not from a static world. If life and matter do not move then functions of earth ceases so also we who would have perished long back. If there is no dynamism, thoughts are obsolete.

Look at the dog you own. Its thinking is only to survive, that is why it is very much attached to you but you are totally independent and your thoughts are more refined to live, to move, to serve, to earn, to take care, etc. This is possible because of extra new frontal brain, which you possess when compared to the dog. A dog has no such new brain (if it has, it is small). Man's thoughts are reasoned, rationalised, logic oriented, processes and executes. These things are possible only when awareness is present and this is not possible when someone is in drowsy state. This is exactly what happens at 'You are in front of your plate at two pm at home.' Somebody is there to give you a plate. You need not think of the plate; automatically you are in front of the plate. If you are not in front of the plate your cognitive centres are drowsy. Therefore, the awakening centre is not functioning, hence drowsy. To sit in front of the plate is automatic hence conditioned. The same gets converted into obsession of eating and you keep grow fatter and fatter.

You look sick, that is the reason why your awakening helps you to be lovely, stand then walk to get the plate, do not wait for somebody to get you the plate. Be active and from this you look healthy bodily and mentally.

When away from home, finding the plate is exactly the opposite. You are more awake, you run here and there to get a plate, your satiety centres do not listen to you. If you are awake then only these centres can be satisfied. For this you have to work hard, keep moving, you cannot be lazy. In finding the plate and searching you look healthy and more alert. In this alertness you do not look sick, you look six packs, ladies come behind you and *KHAN'S* envies you.

"Obsessed You Starve," look at the tragedy and it is a paradox. In the first instance it is automatic with no wakefulness leads to obsessive eating with disease. Now it is a real obsession, obsession of dirt, obsession of no cleanliness, obsession of germs, etc. lead to once again the disease. You are extraordinarily wakeful, vigilant and your eyes become microscopic. Hence, even if you find the plate, because of this double obsession, you suffer and your stomach is not full. When your stomach is not full how can your mind be full? And when you are not full, all the problems start, frustration creeps in, you become fidgety, restless and you are irritable. Obsession with minimal awakening is good for your health but obsession with extraordinary wakeful state is bad for you. It becomes a disease. So be contended.

"Innocent You Are Full," see the funny part of this statement. Everyone likes a child because the child is innocent and God-like. Have you seen a child playing? The child does not differentiate between germs and dirt, keeps everything to mouth. The mother restricts. This child possesses required immunity and does not suffer later on, but your child suffers because of your restrictions. The child is calm when does not interfered with but we are not calm because we are not child-like, we are always childish. You have to be innocent and still like a child; stillness leads to emptiness, in that state everything goes inside and obsessions are out of your mind. After obsessions are out, stomach becomes full, so also your mind. What is the *Manthra?* It is the *Manthra* of acceptance, *Manthra* of *Parivarthana,* to be full and to be happy. If you reach this state, you are liberated a little, you can feel the bliss, and then you enjoy the *Ananda* (happiness). In this happiness, your outlook looks mystique.

DIAMOND WATCH

Truth is elusive and special. It never appears as truth because once the truth goes inside the mind, it gets coloured. Once it gets coloured or painted, then truth becomes valueless. Truth can be valued only when it gets painted with compassion. Is it possible to change? It is possible only with an illuminated mind. Look deeply in to this preamble.

There was a big gathering consisting of persons of all walks of life to hear the preaching by a simple preacher who appeared like *Buddha.* One man in the crowd opposite to the preacher kept lifting his right hand as though he would caress his hair. It appeared like a mannerism but it was not so. This man being rich and famous wanted to seek the attention of the preacher and also from the people who had gathered there to hear the *Pravachana* (spiritual talk). The very idea of him was to show the costliest watch studded with diamonds, which he was wearing. Preacher got annoyed about his antiques and compulsions, which had overridden the simplicity. This preacher walked to him and asked him to submit his watch. Man was happy as he got recognised instantly in the crowd; he got up, did *Sastanga Namaskara* (falling to the ground in front of preacher), looked around and handed over his costliest watch to this preacher. Man's ego got doubled as he became a hero in the crowd instantly. The preacher could make out his mind, consciously enjoyed his ignorance silently. The preacher kept on explaining the beauty of his watch, number of diamonds this watch had, platinum it possessed, company make, and so on and so forth. Man's ego swelled threefold. Almost it took half an hour by the preacher to explain the anatomy of that priced watch. All of a sudden preacher became villain as he took a U-turn who exclaimed this priced watch did not possess any value. Man got a thunder bolt from the sky who got astonished, what was this preacher saying? His watch had no value? He opened his mouth, grabbed his left chest with right hand and got awakened and shaken to listen to the preacher what he would say further. He went on explaining in his *Vedanthic* tone that the watch, which he was holding, had no existence. People asked how? Preacher took all his patience to answer the questions put by his followers. He kept that watch on the table, asked all of them to take an image of that watch in their minds. Crowds in thousands took the image of that watch in their minds. After one minute the preacher gazed at the crowd and asked "Is there any scientist in this crowd?" A Scientist stood up; preacher asked him, "What image you had and what do you think of this watch?" The scientist said, "It is just a watch." The truth was, this scientist never bothered about the value it had, he forgot the diamonds and precious metals it had but he bothered about future inventions, invention of time machine. A Romeo in the crowd forgot everything except how he would offer this watch to his Juliet. A gold smith in that crowd forgot everything and he would think how best he could improve the design of the watch. A thief forgot everything and he would think how he would steal the watch. Likewise, a wealthy man forgot everything and thought how he would possess this watch, and so on and so forth. When there were different versions of this precious watch after entering the different minds painted with different colours, the preacher explained that there is no commonness in the imagination of the peoples' mind who have gathered there, so watch was only a watch as an object in two dimensions which no one could change but in its true sense as the image of watch though seemingly similar in all minds but its version and thinking differed. Hence, as per the preacher, true existence of the watch by all means was verily lost hence the value of this priced watch is zero under *Vedanthic* terms. The man who was hearing to the preacher's formula realised the truth who then got enlightened. He took his watch from the preacher, bowed to the preacher ten times, went out of the crowd without notice. Probably he decided to keep his precious watch in his locker not to open there after.

The preacher explained to the gathering after the man left "Dear friends, tell me now, whether that watch has any existence? It can exist only when all our minds paint with one colour, here there are innumerable different colours, hence it does not possess the truth. The truth is only for the Mr Possessor. For others it is just a show piece with no substance in that, it can be valued only when it is coloured with paint and that paint is colour of love or otherwise colour of compassion. In *Yogic Suthra* the mind coloured by the Knower or *Purusha* is only to known that, it is all apprehending, including or excluding."

PLASTIC

"Special earlier, now the same special is disastrous special, why?" Please explain doctor.

Science has contributed much to the humans. It is unfortunate that we have no photo frames of our past scientists in our homes. We have God and Goddesses in the frames. We are very mean in not remembering such great scientists. In our day-to-day life we use and follow their contributions or inventions but we fail to thank such great people. Their inventions today are basic necessities. We are living and living happily because of pasteurisation, immunisation, phone, electric bulb, motor vehicles, and so on and so forth. But, there are other inventions which were called special in those days and the same has done disastrous effects now. One such invention is the plastic. Plastic bags during those days were special; possessing such plastic was a luxury for us. The same luxury plastic goods and materials usage in our country now led to disastrous effects. It has choked our financial city; it gags and asphyxiated our Mother earth. In west they adopted good disposal system but in our country it is opposite as plastic is stew all over. Plastic do not allow mother earth to drink water. Today our mother earth is devoid of her clothes instead we are allowing her to wear plastic. How can She sustain this onslaught? One day, She would look angrily at her children and She would definitely make her children suffer. These special groups of scientists are real troublemakers. They invent special new machines, which lead to disastrous consequences especially for the innocent and ignorant sections of the society. Today you name something new and it has its own problem. The communication and the media are also fallen to this group. How can this disastrous special be made special? This is possible only by us. Use plastic wherever it is necessary, and dispose it properly. Communication is essential, but do not abuse it. Media is knowledge oriented, not for pleasure. By following these principles, we can make our country to more special. This is what I want to tell special should not become disastrous special.

BLACK BEAUTY

It was a sweltering summer; temperature was soaring at 40 degree Celsius. My good friend a lawyer by profession was wearing his usual customary black suit and wearing dark cooling glass. He was smart looking in spite of his black colour. I was curious to know whether in this temperature was it necessary for a lawyer friend to wear black suit. I questioned him about the reason behind wearing this black suit. He failed to give a suitable answer to me. One day it came like a flash, why lawyer should wear black suit? What is the symbolic meaning behind such a black suit? This is just my theory but I may be wrong. If I go a little deep into this uniform I see some amazing reasons. Actually, the black suit is a nuisance, already sweating and he sweats double. Black colour absorbs heat but it does not absorb signals. This is exactly the reason why a lawyer wear black suit. The client approaches lawyer to plead justice on behalf of him. A lawyer has to be extraordinarily precise in hearing and summarising his client's complaints. Now let us say the lawyer wears any other colour except black, this colour would absorb all the signals, which was emitted by his client. Wearing black colour by the lawyer would just repel such signals, which are unwanted. The luring signals emit by the opposite sex client are well controlled by black colour which covers him total. Hence wearing such black suit by the lawyer makes him more attentive while listening to his client. In these state lawyers *Panchendriyas* (our five senses) are under his control. Lawyer's *Shravana* (hearing) improves. Hence, their *Manana* (understanding) is at all-time high to know their client better.

What about his tie, which is white in colour? This colour all over the world is symbolically known for the compassion. This tie tucked nearer to a lawyer's heart. This tie's white colour has a special power of absorbing warmth. Nuns, reverend fathers and nurses all over the world wear white clothes who are known for their compassion and forgiveness. Without this white tie the lawyer's attentiveness is at the lowest ebb. This means that his understanding and reasoning of the client's complaint will not be to the highest levels. The same signals in the form of warmth what he perceives through the white tie from the grieving client go directly from lawyer's heart to his brain. Hence, the signals he perceived from his client would get refined by this way. It is like doubly saturated edible oil, which has no effect on the heart. In the same fashion, these refined signals would enable the solicitor to comprehend client's agony better, reasoning and summarising would be easier, thoughts are valued when he faces his case in front of the judge while arguing on behalf of his client. The judge would be happy to understand the deliberations and gives a better judgment after hearing both sides. Now black suit, suits a lawyer to enhance his compassionate perception. Here white tie means, not just a piece of attraction but keeps the heart open for all his clients who are at the mercy of the solicitor to seek their justice. This is the essence of wearing black suit; hence, I call them black beauties.

SHAKA SHAKA BABY

Why people are scared to see a psychiatrist? Apart from ignorance it is wildly seen that the psychiatrists as doctors who drugs the patient lifelong. It is a myth, not true but I have seen patients who visit a psychiatrist and take drugs for their life without consulting or coming for follow up just like alcohol or *Gutka* (beetle nut with additives) consumption. Is it the fault of a psychiatrist? Our drugs are psycho corrective drugs and once the illnesses are cured or controlled, drugs are tapered down and stopped. This depends on the treating psychiatrist. I have seen few physicians who prescribe antipsychotics for agitation in depression and mean while they totally forgets their patients. Agitation is a common symptom in agitated endogenous depression. This depressive patient who requires antidepressants gets antipsychotic for their life time and lands up with no *Shaka Shaka Baby.* Constantly this patient is under *Neurolepsia* (muscle tightness). The people around him are happy, because after the tablets he is *Buddha* like. But in actuality we have taken out his good days of work, his further progress, his family suffers and would go in to shambles and care of his children affected. This is one side of the coin. A patient with chronic schizophrenia looks depressed. Here few physicians try their antidepressants and the same old story repeats; months pass by, again no *Shaka Shaka Baby.* The patients have been asked to wear once again strait jackets by few physicians. Recently to avoid this confusion, researchers and pharmaceutical companies have come with a naïve idea. New drugs have been researched and tried to take care of psychosis as well as depression. Hence, few physicians' job becomes easy, hence, these doctors can shake their purse and patients can shake their body.

SHRINK

A psychiatrist in the west is called shrink but in the east he is not called so. Days are not so far away to call psychiatrists shrinking. Yes, am I shrinking? Look at the paradox, shrink and shrinking. Let me explain shrinking rather than shrink because actually speaking I do not know what westerns mean by this word 'shrink.' I am sure psychiatrists are shrinking but why only psychiatrists, members of all medical fraternity as such are shrinking. Not by height, but with their knowledge. We should thank for our super inventions of information technology. It is the speed of accessing to the medical information, which made the medical field to shrink. If this is true, why there should be a medical degree or a post-graduate degree? A little experience can make a person doctor. That is how compounders have become flourishing doctors. Something high like precise surgical procedures requires practice. Sorry to say this that our education system is shrinking and also our learning is dissipating. Students now go to medical college only to seek a degree but not to imbibe and learn medicine proper. New inventions like radiological diagnostic software's in CAT, MRI, FRMI, PET, SPECT, etc. take care of all problems of medical students. Now interaction is between patient and machine rather than with doctor and patient. The health ministry is magnanimous enough to increase the number of seats at under-graduation level and also at post-graduation levels. Government wants to fill doctors and patients' ratio in future but at what cost? A good number of passing percentage with medical students is increasing and simultaneously their learning is also decreasing. Today everything is available in internet. That is how doctor's focus is on searching the search engines. The doctor's focus on a patient has gone. The doctor's knowledge is assessed through the number of patients he sees but not by the time he spends. Today's world is mechanical and doctors are robots. When we observe the district government hospitals, patients just flock around the doctor like sheep. Because of less time and minimal doctor's number, what type of knowledge doctor can try on his patients? Today doctors listening to patients' problems have gone and it is done with machines and computers. This is really a tragedy or unfortunate. Fine, our world is moving at a fast pace but in which direction is the question. In the process of searching, the surfer who searches medicine in search engines does internet provides relief to his patient? Earlier psychiatrists view mental illness was more of a subjective subject. Now the trend has changed and it is more of an objective one and as such psychiatry has become object-oriented hence automatically today demand for psychiatry is increasing. Today techies have become doctors. Ultimately patients and their bystanders are at the losing end. People ask doctors whether the doctor possesses a laptop with internet access because they have lost faith with a treating doctor. Self-management is the new avatar today. This tendency has its own problems. Because of this, people's health is shrinking so also with the doctors as their knowledge is shrinking. There are no teachers today, leave alone masters. This is the reason why medical knowledge of the students is shrinking because of insufficient involvement from teachers.

This does not mean that there are no good teachers. Definitely wonderful teachers are there but by and large we lack the good teaching techniques. When this was enquired by the students to their teachers they would take the *Pathanjali* book and show *Kriya Yoga Suthra*, which says *Thapas, Swadhyaya* and *Eshwarapranidhanaha* are the hallmarks of learning. If a student asks about teaching, teachers have a beautiful placard written up in colourful words *Swadhyaya.* This means self-study. This is the reason why I tell we are all 'shrinking' in our knowledge and also failing in taking care of the patients.

How to get away from this? Simple, one has to expand. I asked one of my friends who is a pundit in psychiatry who could not answer my question. As I was pestering him to answer, he got tired of me and said "You fellow, go and jump into a pond." Exactly this is what happens with many students as they could not find any answer to their problems in this world. They shrink and disappear to a point of no return. Paradox is that, the pundit does not know that the jump into a pond full of water would cause lungs to expand, life to shrink. Let us not take this statement literally. Watch what I am going to explain, read carefully and this is a type of meditative technique. I used this and got expanded not by my body but by my mind. Master says, "Watch the pond at mid night and this pond just glows under moon. It is a mirror reflecting your image, it is wonderful to watch, and on this, you realise and understand. Do not verbalise, be silent, be looking to the pond, when you look in silence you observe. Try this—to the undisturbed serene mirror like water, throw a marble, do not use force to throw, throw the marble as children throw, not to the periphery, to the centre and all our problems are because of periphery. Periphery always gets attached to the great *Maya* that is how we are not central. Observe the centre, and listen to the music. Disturbance after throwing the marble produces music and this music has wavelengths, which are expanding from small waves to large waves, and in this charm of dance, you find your mind expanding. This type of understanding and learning the art of music converts a teacher into master." This is the eastern way of teaching. That is why I tell all my friends, masters are difficult to find because eastern techniques are forgotten. Psychiatry is wonderful and all evidence based and whatever we find presently in psychiatry textbooks are of the western type. By mixing the east and the west, psychiatry is like an ocean of knowledge, if this ocean is undisturbed it is flat, disturb it and find the music and dance. West is available in the internet but not the east, because it is mystique and learning mysticism is like Harry Potter. When these two, east and west mix, then psychiatrists are not called shrink instead they are called expanding. Expansion with mind is like *Megha* or cloud, in that state we are floating and happier.

Try the technique that I have explained, if you win, you are not called "shrink."

ACTOR

Doctor you said on the other day "Heroes are there everywhere" What does actually this statement would mean to you Doctor?

You asked an interesting question. Have you heard of *Meru Nata? Meru* means 'above all' and *Nata* means 'actor' in Kannada language. They are our vintage heroes. Everyone expects to become such type of heroes. In actuality, we do not know what pain they had possessed inside them but being an actor's they wanted to act so that people would emulate acting qualities. Their acting is natural from their heart, they have no coach and their acting comes from within or otherwise from centre. Because of all these qualities, they are real heroes of ester years. They are colourful, talented and also exhibitionists which our cameras just suck superficial acting and beam out their art through movies and television. What we actually see them is more from their periphery but not from their centre like in staged epic dramas. Earlier there were only movies and no television but today only television as old theatres are getting converted in to malls. There are many television channels but no true actors. But, still these 24/7 television channels should work; otherwise employees of TV companies go for starving. Hence, you see repetitions one in half an hour and if we are not TV addicts, we virtually vomit. Somehow, channels have to survive through their TRP. Hence, they have to keep on picking up heroes all the time but such yester heroes hardly we see today. Hence, actors whom they get are from the periphery, not from the true dramas they had played, so no true actors now. Kindly follow this paradox. A villain in action is only available in movies but a villain of no action is available in television. In this present circumstance, there are innumerable instantaneous heroes. They are heroes of corruption, heroes of murder, heroes of rape, heroes of cheating and so and so forth. Because of this reason, 24/7 channels are full and channels beams relentlessly all days and nights. How many heroes you want today? I do not call them villain because what is the authenticity? He has to be proved beyond doubt by judiciary. Hence, they are all masked and they look like Phantom in their mask. In this world we have numerous unsung heroes' but they do not come to the limelight. The reason for this is that they are not colourful. Present hero's colours are well illuminated with artificial lights. These illuminations are well picked up by our ever-present cameras. Our science is still backward, our cameras are outdated and we boast 3D but in order to pick up or shoot unsung heroes we require multidimensional cameras. Presently our scientists have not discovered such cameras to pick-up such actors because present movie cameras are unable to penetrate the centre. Present cameras don't pick up the light illuminated by *"Prathibha* (enlightened light)*."* This *Prathibha* actually illuminate great person's colour of passion and compassion, which our present cameras fail to pick up. Even if we try to shoot them with such cameras, they shut their door instantaneously because of the innate shyness of these cameras in front of these great people. Such illuminated heroes just explained are there everywhere, present all over, but they are locked and blocked for us to see.

MANIPULATION

"Manipulation," what is your view doctor?

This is a good question. The economy of any country stands on its transparency, not on manipulation. The west believed in this transparency. Therefore, its economy is said to be sound but it may not sound the same for some other countries. Ours is a developing country. In this development, our intelligence also has developed and it has grown up leaps and bounds, like quantum jump. With changing and developing intelligence, problems kept on increasing. It is the issue of Govt but coming to the point of manipulation, egoistic intelligence is the hallmark of an HOD (Head of the department) in any institute or university, which is actually a barrier for any student to update his knowledge; student is scared to interact or even to look at his HOD. The HOD never allows their students to manipulate but today still all dissertations lack the standard and are of worthless quality. But, somehow PhDs and PGs (post-graduation) are offered to students by many universities. If these universities do not issue such certificates our country would choke due to the lack of quality teachers. As there is a dearth of teachers, automatically we do not find masters. If there are no manipulations in the university then you find only the masters, as of now no masters but only teachers, hence manipulation is rampant. Our economy is not a transparent economy but manipulated economy. Companies pay rosy salaries for IIM (Indian institute of management) new comers to manipulate their accounts.

By looking at the company projections people flock to buy shares, rise in the share actually artificial or cooked up prices. In reality, the shareholder in the long run may not burn his fingers but today people's attitude is to make fast buck that is how they burn their fingers. There are good companies like good doctors but one should be lucky to find such companies. The same is true with the student who is lucky enough to have good teacher or master. One student asked a known distant professor about the manipulation, that professor yelled at his ward over phone with his full throttle "You fool what do you think, can you talk to a HOD like this? You dirty fellow." It is not his problem, it is his ego which is reflecting the poor professor who does not know how this world standing today. This world is standing only on manipulations. The ego does not accept the reality. Hence professors lacks realisation. That is how students are scared to talk with them because they are busy within the four walls of the university chamber. In a family, a wife manipulates to get the favour by her husband, husband also does same and children do all tricks of manipulations to find innumerable comforts from their parents. So the story of manipulation in this world keeps going on and on which cannot be stopped unless there is something called self-realisation, *Sakshi Bhava* (self-witness) works or comes in to picture. This is possible only when one bends and finds a U-turn like Buddha. After all Buddha's teaching is to move, flow and change. We are moving, there is a jerky flow rather than smooth flow, change is there but not for the good but only for the bad and manipulation is there in this world only for negativity and not for positivity. Anyway, we have to move forward positively to have good physical and mental health and in turn to aspire for a *Rama Rajya* (good governance) in our country.